PROJECT 2000

in eas

JOHN CARROLL

**COMPUTER
STEP**

In easy steps is an imprint of Computer Step
Southfield Road . Southam
Warwickshire CV47 OFB . England

http://www.ineasysteps.com

Notice of Liability
Every effort has been made to ensure that this book contains accurate and current information. However, Computer Step and the author shall not be liable for any loss or damage suffered by readers as a result of any information contained herein.

Trademarks
Microsoft® and Windows® are registered trademarks of Microsoft Corporation. All other trademarks are acknowledged as belonging to their respective companies.

Printed and bound in the United Kingdom

ISBN 1-84078-114-9

Contents

Adding Structure   57

4

More About Tasks   73

5

Resources   83

6

Hyperlinks and the Web

15

Network Diagrams

16

Programme Management

17

Project Central

18

The Basics

This chapter explains what Microsoft Project 2000 is and how it can help you to manage your project. It provides some background to projects and project management and then introduces the main features of Project 2000.

Covers

Chapter One

Introduction

Microsoft Project 2000 is a great project management tool. Managing projects can be a complex activity but, with the help of Project 2000, you can plan, schedule and control the progress of your project.

Why do you need to plan and control your project? Well, statistically, around 50% of business projects are not successful. If you don't plan and control your project, the chances are that it will be among that 50%!

This book covers Project 2000. If you have an earlier version of Microsoft Project some of the features may not be available or may be slightly different.

Whether your project is a simple short-term one (such as arranging a company meeting) or a more complex project (like developing a new computer system), Project 2000 will let you stay in control.

Used as a planning tool, Project 2000 can produce some great looking charts to help you plan your project. But Project can do a lot more besides:

- It can help you allocate and schedule work, tasks and activities.

- It can produce a critical path analysis to identify where you will need to track progress carefully.

- It can identify if you have too much work allocated to any one person.

- It can schedule facilities such as meeting rooms and overhead projectors for you.

- It can interface with your e-mail system or Internet browser to allow you to keep your team in the picture.

- It can publish to the Web using HTML and export files to Excel so you can produce charts and graphs of your project's progress.

And with the addition of Project Central (a companion product) you can run your projects across an Intranet or the Web.

How to Use This Book

Each topic in this book is intended to be free standing in its own right and you can just pick the topics you are interested in. If, however, you want to use it in a more structured way, the following are some general guidelines if you are not sure exactly where to begin.

If you're new to Project Management

Start at the beginning and work right the way through to Chapter 11. Use our example project to build up experience and test things and try them out as you go. Then go back to Chapter 2 and begin again with your real project for the maximum benefit.

If you're new to Project 2000 (but not to project management)

If you've used another project planning tool, then skim through Chapters 1 and 2 and start at Chapter 3 (the examples should illustrate any differences). If you've not used another project planning tool, then work through from Chapter 1 (but skim the topics on project management).

If you've used a previous version of Microsoft Project

Read 'What's New in Project 2000' (the next topic) and skim the remainder of this chapter and Chapter 2, then work through from Chapter 3 looking out for the new features. In particular read the chapter on Project Central as this is a completely new companion product to Project 2000.

If you use 2 July 2001 as the start date for your exercise project your results should be exactly the same as the illustrations in this book.

The exercises

The exercises through this book build up a project plan step-by-step.

The later topics build on the project and assume that you have saved it at the end of the previous topic. But don't worry if you have skipped any topics or chapters, you should be able to see from the screen shots what's happening and be able to recreate them. If not just go back to the previous topic and follow the steps there.

What's New in Project 2000?

New Features

There are a number of quite significant enhancements in Project 2000, compared to the previous version. The major new features are as follows:

Grouping

You can now set up your own custom groups of tasks (or resources) and view them rolled up in place of the regular summary tasks. They can also be displayed using selected fonts and a range of colour bands for ease of viewing.

Outline Codes

You can now define your own outline codes rather than having them created based on the standard outline structure of the project. This allows a project to be structured along cost code or organisational lines.

Graphical Indicators

'Traffic lights' can be associated with the data in a custom field in order to highlight potential problems such as budget or time overrun.

Fiscal Year

Organisations that do not use the standard calendar year can now define and use a fiscal year for major and minor timescales in any combination.

Task Calendars

Where a task can only occur on certain days or at certain times, you can now create a task-specific calendar for it.

Materials Resources

The new 'Type of Resource' field can be used to define consumable material resources (such as paint) if required with a fixed or variable cost.

Deadline Dates

In addition to being able to apply constraints, this new field allows you to set deadline dates and have Project 2000 highlight any that cannot be met.

Custom Field Value Lists

User-defined pick lists can be set up to restrict the values that can be entered and simplify entry of custom data.

Calculations in Custom Fields

You can now place formulae in custom fields (similar to Excel) to manipulate and perform calculations on numeric, flag, date and text data.

OLE DB

Other applications can now access (read only) the Project 2000 database to integrate project data with other applications.

Estimated Task Duration

You can now indicate that the duration of a task is estimated and change it to be confirmed at a later date.

Month Duration

Months are now supported as a unit of duration.

Contoured Resource Availability

The percentage resource availability can now be varied from period to period to allow for variations in availability.

Clear Baseline

You can now clear the baseline or interim plan for selected tasks or the whole project.

Adaptive Menus

As in Office 2000, the most often used menu items are featured more prominently on the drop down menus, which can also be expanded to show all menu options.

Templates

Project templates can now be set up and used for new projects in a similar way to other Microsoft Office applications.

Variable Row Height

Individual rows can have their borders dragged to vary their height.

AutoSave
Project 2000 can now automatically save a project at chosen time intervals and also prompt you before saving if required.

Office Server Extensions Support
You can now save files to Web servers in the same way as to File servers.

Single Document Interface
Switching between projects and other tasks is now simplified as each project is an entry on the task bar.

Default Save Path and Format
You can specify a default save path and also a save format (such as Project 98 for compatibility purposes).

Accessibility
Project 2000 supports third-party accessibility aids through Microsoft Active Accessibility interfaces.

Install on Demand
Project 2000 has the option to only install the components users need, as and when they need them.

Roaming User Support
Users can log on to any PC on a network and maintain their own settings and preferences.

Windows Terminal Server Support
Project 2000 can run on a Terminal server.

COM Add-ins
Project 2000 supports COM Add-ins to extend functionality.

Project Central
Project Central is a new companion product that allows the project manager to distribute information to a project team and solicit input from them over a company Intranet or even the World Wide Web.

Improvements to existing features

In addition to the new features listed, there are a number of improvements to existing features:

Network Diagram (Formerly the PERT Chart)

You can now customise network diagrams with new filtering and layout options, formatting features and box styles.

Rollup Gantt

You can now display bars for each sub task on a single summary line (in place of the standard rolled-up bar).

Task Outline Level

The new Show button on the Formatting toolbar makes it easier to expand and collapse the outline structure to the required level.

Cross-Project Critical Path

You can calculate a single critical path across all sub-projects in a consolidated project.

Task and Project Priority

You can now set priority levels from 1 to 1,000 both for tasks and for projects.

Scaling and Printing

New and improved scaling (to fit) and printing options give better control over printing of documents.

Copy Picture

Higher quality images, larger sizes and better scaling.

HTML Help

Microsoft's new standard Help engine has been implemented which also allows the help pages to be customised.

Technical Improvements

The Hyperlink dialogue box, database performance, resource pooling, inserted projects, event handling and Visual Basic for Applications (VBA) have all been improved.

Installing Project 2000

Although 30MB of free space is the requirement for the typical installation, you will need more space if you wish to install some of the options under the custom installation. Try to start with 100MB or more of free space. The Setup program will warn you if you do not have enough room.

Installing Project 2000 is done by running the program SETUP.EXE. If you have a CD-ROM version, this usually runs automatically when the CD is inserted into the drive.

Before running SETUP, make sure you have a suitable system. You need a PC with the following:

- Pentium class processor running at 75MHz or higher.

- At least 24MB of RAM (memory) on Windows 95/98 or 40MB on Windows NT/2000.

- At least 30MB of free disk space for a typical installation.

- A CD-ROM drive.

To install Project Central you will need a file server running Windows NT4.0 Server (Service Pack 4) or later. To install Project Central Client you will need another 10-20MB of free disk space in addition to the above.

If you are going to continue using an earlier version of Microsoft Project as well as Project 2000 you will need to change the default install directory:

When installing large programs, it is easy to use almost all the space on your hard disk. Unfortunately, Windows needs free space for temporary files. You also need to allow space for your documents. It is best to keep 100MB or more free at all times.

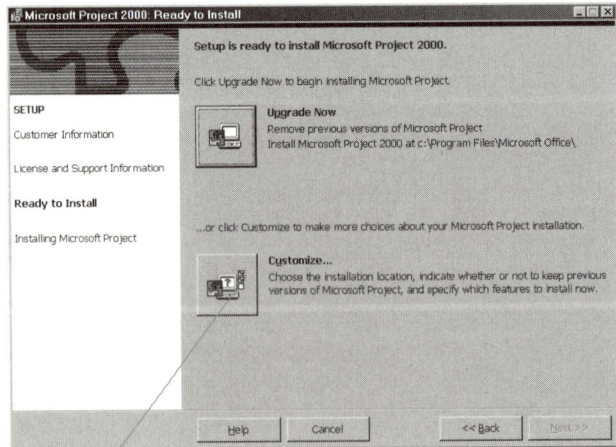

Click the Customize button.

Next, Setup asks you which directory to install into:

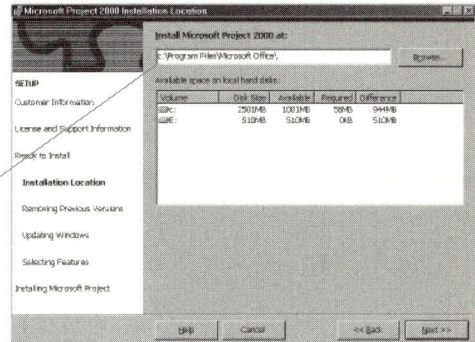

2 Type the name of the directory you want to install Project 2000 in.

The default for Project 2000 is to remove any previous versions of Microsoft Project that it finds. You therefore need to override this default:

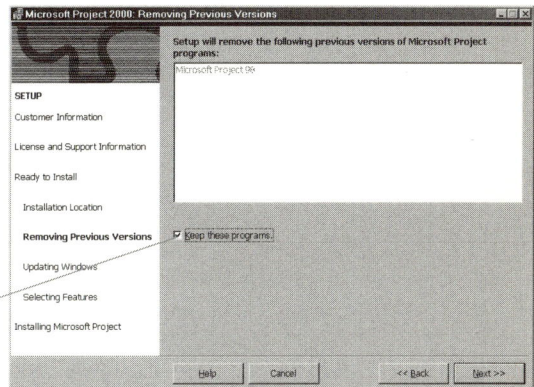

3 Check this box to keep any required previous versions.

Project 2000 will then continue and complete the installation.

The first time you open Project 2000 a Planning Wizard will appear asking if you want to copy your global settings from the previous version of Microsoft Project. This will import any changes you have made to customise Project 98. It will not be able to import any changes to earlier versions.

What is a Project?

A project is a controlled process designed to achieve an identified objective. The objective could be a personal one such as organising a foreign trip, a construction project like building a house, or a business project like implementing a new accounting system.

Whatever sort of project you have, there are three key characteristics that you can associate with it:

1. It must have an end result or outcome. There would be no point in carrying out a project if it did not achieve anything. Further, the end result must be wanted or have some sort of benefit; if not, there would be no point doing it.

2. It has to have a beginning or be initiated. Projects do not happen spontaneously, they need to be kicked off. But this step must come after the end result has been defined. If you were to initiate a project without knowing what you wanted to achieve, you would be likely to go round in ever decreasing circles!

3. It has to be carried out – the middle bit, getting from A to B. Again, things do not happen automatically just because you have defined your end result and initiated a project. The hard work comes in getting the project *successfully* from A to B.

Whatever your project is, Project 2000 can help you reach your objective successfully.

Project Management

Projects need to be managed if they are going to be successful. So, is project management the same thing as ordinary management?

Ordinary management is involved with managing a process. It could be a department issuing invoices. It could be a factory producing widgets. It could be a telephone call centre. Whatever it is, managing it is a continuous process. Unless they go out of business, the department will continue issuing invoices, the factory will continue producing widgets and the call centre will continue dealing with calls.

On the other hand, a project begins when it is initiated and ends when it has achieved its goal. It has a finite life. Project management is the management of change.

The Project Manager's role is to steer the project successfully from its beginning to its end and deal with anything that happens along the way.

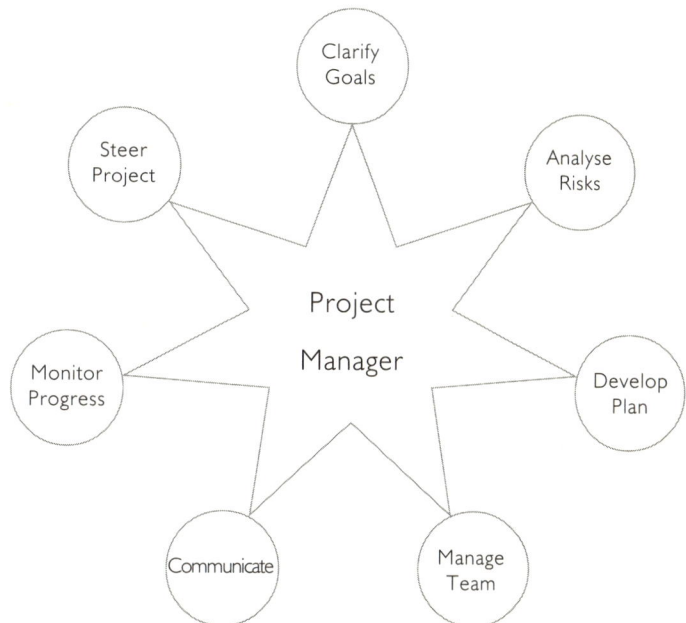

The Gantt Chart

The first thing you see when you open or create a new project is the Gantt chart.

It is the default view, and with good reason. The Gantt chart is probably the most widely used and most useful project management tool.

They say that every picture tells a thousand words – this is the key picture in your project.

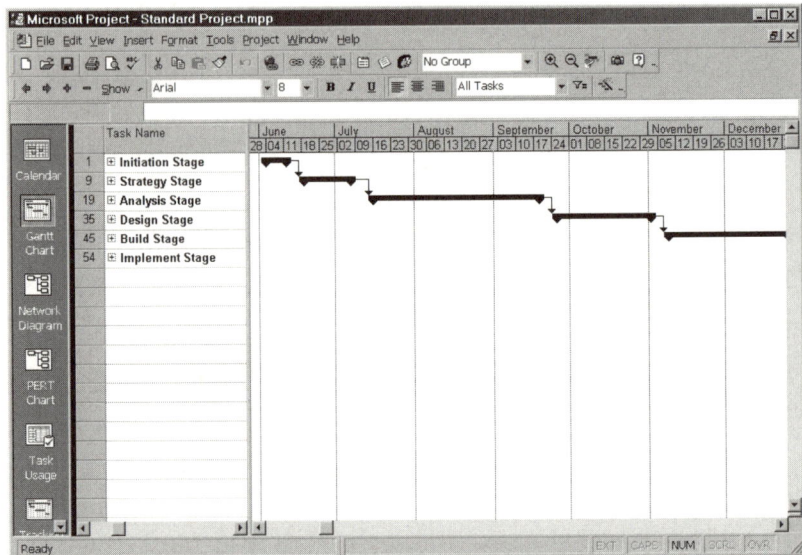

At the summary level (as shown above) you can view the whole project on one screen or on one sheet of paper. The Gantt chart represents the most frequently used way of representing a project graphically and is particularly useful for senior management in its rolled-up summary form.

The Gantt chart view is more than just a view, though. It also allows you to plan and control your project by inserting and editing project tasks, setting and changing project milestones and even allocating and controlling project resources.

Tasks and Milestones

At the detailed level in Gantt chart view, you can view the individual Tasks and Project Milestones:

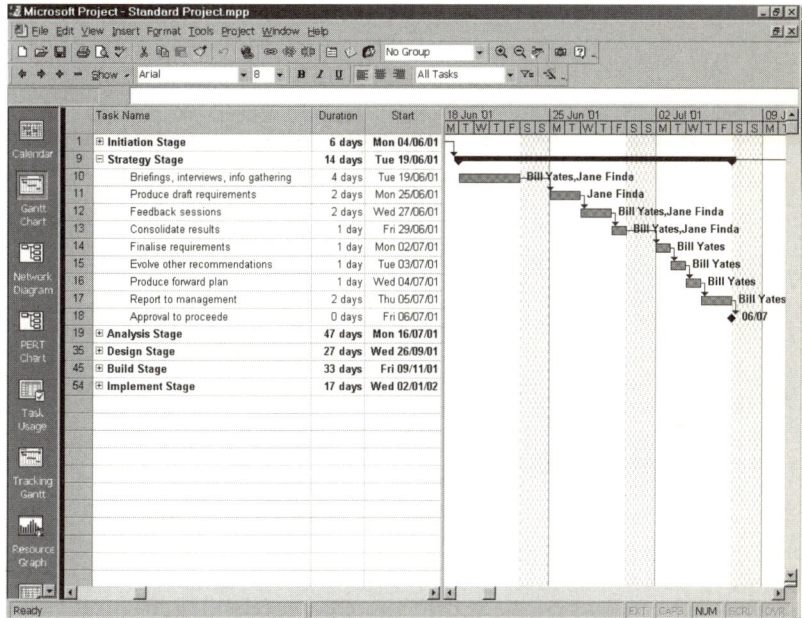

In Gantt Chart view you can:

- Expand or close up the list of tasks by clicking on the '+' or '-' beside any summary task or using the buttons on the Formatting Toolbar.

- See and edit the scheduled start date, duration and finish date for individual tasks.

- See and edit the linkages and dependencies between tasks.

- Set and change your project milestones.

- See who is allocated to each task and, if necessary, allocate more resources or change the allocation.

Resource Usage

Resources are the people and facilities that you will use on your project. You can track resource usage through both the Task Usage and Resource Usage views.

The Task Usage view allows you to see who and what is being used on each Task:

While the Resource Usage view allows you to see what each person is doing:

Resource Usage view enables you to monitor work assignments, identify potential problems through overload and generally stay in firm control of your project.

View Bar

While the Gantt Chart view is the default (and probably the most useful) view in Project 2000, there are another 25 pre-defined views. These can be selected through the View Bar.

HOT TIP

Although there are already 26 views in Project 2000, you can still create additional custom views of your own.

The View Bar

HOT TIP

The View Bar can be hidden to give you more room for your chart by clicking View>View Bar on the Menu Bar. To bring it back just click View>View Bar again (a tick reappears next to View Bar in the drop-down menu).

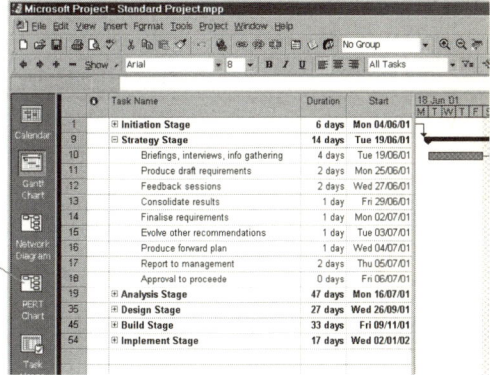

The View Bar can be used to switch back and forth between views. These are the views and their icons:

	Calendar:	a monthly calendar showing tasks and their duration.
	Gantt Chart:	the default view of tasks and time.
	Network Diagram:	a chart of tasks showing their links and dependencies.
	Task Usage:	tasks and who is allocated to them.
	Tracking Gantt:	shows actual against scheduled.
	Resource Graph:	shows usage or cost of a resource over time.
	Resource Sheet:	shows details of each resource.
	Resource Usage:	shows a list of task assignments by resource.
	More Views:	gives the full list of all 26 available views.

Toolbars

The Standard and Formatting Toolbars contain the standard Microsoft Office buttons together with a number of Project 2000 specific ones:

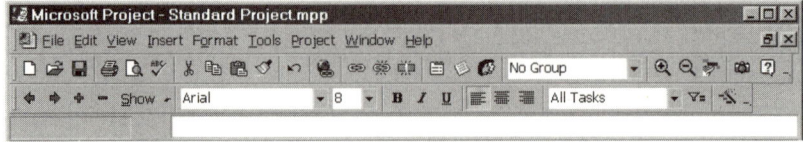

This table omits those icons which are more or less standard to Windows programmes (e.g. Bold and Italic).

(You can always find out what any button does by pausing the mouse pointer over it.)

The buttons are:

Standard

	New Project
	Open
	Save
	Print
	Print preview
	Spell Check
	Cut
	Copy
	Paste
	Format painter
	Undo
	Insert hyperlink
	Link Tasks
	Unlink Tasks
	Split Task
	Information

	Notes
	Assign Resources
	Zoom In
	Zoom out
	Go to selected task
	Chart snapshot
	Help

Formatting

	Outdent
	Indent
	Show Subtasks
	Hide Subtasks
Show	Show options
	Autofilter
	Chart wizard

How to Get Help

There are several ways of getting help in Project 2000.

From the Menu Bar:

1 Select Help>Contents and Index.

2 Select the Contents Tab for a full list of contents, Answer Wizard to type a question or the Index Tab for a searchable Index.

Use the F1 key or click Help on the Button bar to open the Office Assistant.

If you want to know what something is, use Shift+F1 then point and click at the item you want to know about.

1 Type in your question.

2 Click on Search.

You can even get Help from the Web using Help>Office on the Web from the Menu Bar:

1 Make sure you have a Web connection.

2 Click Help on the Menu bar.

3 Click Office on the Web.

Getting Started

For a bit more information about the concepts of project management and an overview of the capabilities of Project 2000, you can take a Quick Preview, a Tutorial or get a Project Map:

1   Select Help from the Menu bar.

2   Select Getting Started.

3   Select Quick Preview, Tutorial or Project Map.

Help	
? Microsoft Project Help	F1
Show the Office Assistant	
Contents and Index	
Getting Started	◄
What's This?	Shift+F1
Office on the Web	
Detect and Repair...	
About Microsoft Project	

Quick Preview
Tutorial
Project Map

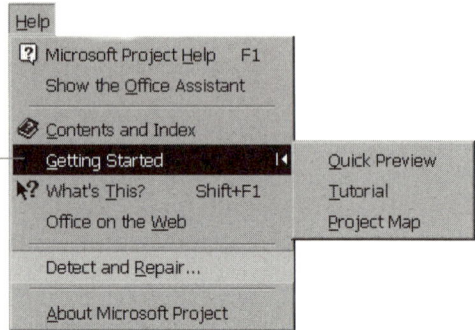

If you select Quick Preview the Welcome dialogue box will open and play. Use Next, Back and Play Again to control the preview.

It is worth while taking a quick look at these features, particularly if you are new to project management.

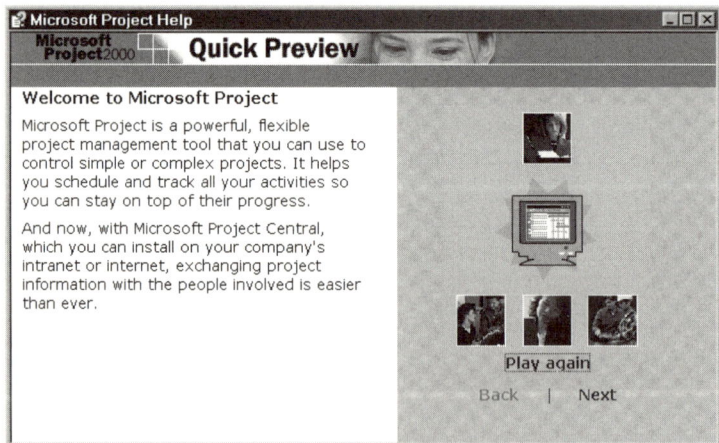

Welcome to Microsoft Project

Microsoft Project is a powerful, flexible project management tool that you can use to control simple or complex projects. It helps you schedule and track all your activities so you can stay on top of their progress.

And now, with Microsoft Project Central, which you can install on your company's intranet or internet, exchanging project information with the people involved is easier than ever.

Play again

Back | Next

The Tutorial will give you a Web-style tutorial on projects, project management and Project 2000. Project Map will give you a Web-style guide through the steps involved in creating a new project in Project 2000.

Managing Your Project

This chapter introduces a structured approach to managing a project and explores the ways in which Project 2000 can help you manage your project.

Covers

Chapter Two

A 4-Step Approach

Project management is the management of change.

In order to manage change and therefore manage your project, you need to carry out a number of steps or tasks.

In 'What is a project?' we defined a project as having a beginning, a middle and an end. If we expand the middle bit (carrying it out) into two steps we will have a 4-step approach to project management:

1 Identify what you are trying to achieve – define your project aims, goals or objectives.

2 Plan how you will get there – once you have identified your project objectives you can begin to map out what you are going to do to achieve them.

3 Carry it out – do it or manage it.

4 Hand it over – once the project is completed you have finished your job.

Experienced project managers may feel this is a simplistic approach. It is, but be patient as we will build on it in later sections.

Interestingly, the difficult step for some project managers is the last one. They find it difficult to let go.

The project manager's job is to implement change. Once that change has been implemented their role as a project manager is completed. The new, changed state becomes a production process and that requires production (rather than project) management.

In the remainder of this chapter we will expand on each of these four steps and look at what is involved, starting with step 1, defining your objectives.

Step 1 – Define Your Objectives

The first step in any project is to define your objectives. You need to define your objectives in order to be able to:

- Make sure you have identified the right target.

- Focus the other members of the project team on what the project is about.

- Create team commitment to and agreement about the project objectives.

- Ensure that you involve all interested parties in achieving a successful project outcome.

When you set out to define your objectives there is a useful acronym to remember: SMART. Objectives need to be: Strategic; Measurable; Agreed; Realistic; and Timed.

Strategic:	your objectives must address some strategic business purpose or need. If they do not, does the project really matter to the business and if not, why carry it out?
Measurable:	if you can't measure the achievement of the project, how will you know if you've achieved anything?
Agreed:	if the rest of the business and the rest of the project team have not agreed with the objectives, there will be no commitment to these objectives.
Realistic:	if the objectives are not realisable, the project team will soon realise that and lose any commitment to the project.
Timed:	if there is no pressure to complete the project it will never get completed.

When you define your objectives, make sure that they are

SMART.

So think about your project objectives now. Have you defined them adequately and are they SMART?

Keep it Simple

Another useful acronym to remember when thinking about your project objectives is KISS. It stands for: Keep It Short and Simple.

Your objectives should not only be SMART, they also need to be brief and simple to understand. If not someone out there will misunderstand them!

If you don't keep it simple, this is a little reminder of what can go wrong:

As Marketing requested it

As Sales ordered it

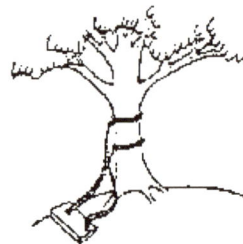

As the analyst designed it

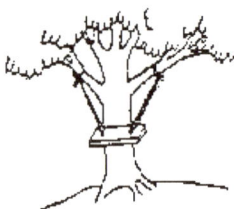

As the programmers developed it

As it was installed

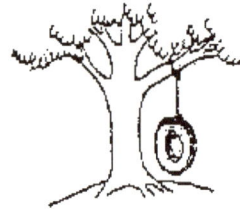

What the customer wanted

So spend some more time making sure that your project objectives are stated simply. Make sure you know what you want to achieve then make sure other people do. The best way of doing that is to show your objectives to other people and ask them for their feedback.

An example:'In order to free up cash for business expansion, the project aims to achieve a reduction in stock holding of 20% by the end of the financial year.' That is a simple objective that is also SMART (if it is realistic and agreed).

Starting a Project

Start Project 2000 by clicking on Start>Programs>Project 2000. Project 2000 opens in Gantt Chart view with a blank project file and you can begin entering information about your project.

The Project Information dialogue box may open automatically when you create a new project. This can be turned on or off from the Tools>Options>General tab.

1 Click Project>Project Information on the Menu Bar. The Project Information dialogue box opens.

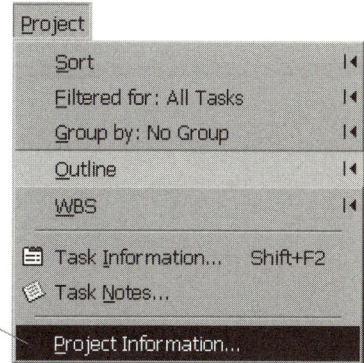

Project	
Sort	◄
Filtered for: All Tasks	◄
Group by: No Group	◄
Outline	◄
WBS	◄
Task Information... Shift+F2	
Task Notes...	
Project Information...	

2 By default, the Start date will be the current date. If you want to change it click the control beside the date box to open a calendar and select the date.

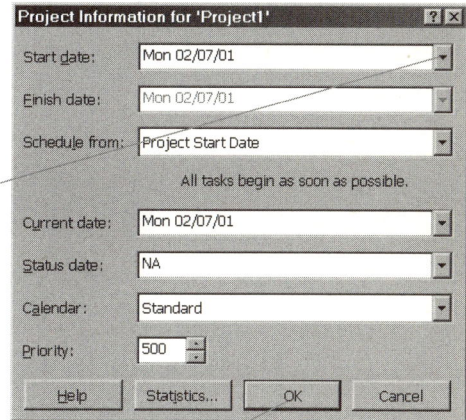

Project Information for 'Project1'

Start date:	Mon 02/07/01
Finish date:	Mon 02/07/01
Schedule from:	Project Start Date
	All tasks begin as soon as possible.
Current date:	Mon 02/07/01
Status date:	NA
Calendar:	Standard
Priority:	500

Help   Statistics...   OK   Cancel

3 When you're happy with your start date, click the OK button.

Scheduling backwards from a finish date is much more difficult and is best avoided until you have some experience of forward scheduling.

By default the project is scheduled forward from the Start date. You can also schedule backwards from a finish date by selecting Schedule from: Project Finish Date and entering your finish date.

Entering Summary Information

Once you've opened your project and set the start date you should enter your objectives and other summary information.

1 Click File>Properties on the Menu Bar and the Project Properties dialogue box opens. Select the Summary tab if not already selected.

2 Type the Title, Subject, your name and your Company name (if relevant).

3 Enter the type of project and keywords that could help locate the file in future.

Project1 Properties

| General | Summary | Statistics | Contents | Custom |

Title: Strategy Study

Subject: Financial Review

Author: Your Name

Manager: Your Name

Company: Your Company Plc

Category: Strategic Review

Keywords: strategy, finance, review

Comments: To carry out a 6 week study in order to determine if there is a business requirement for a new financial accounting system.

Hyperlink base:

Template:

☐ Save preview picture

OK   Cancel

4 Now type your project objectives into the Comments field.

5 Click OK. You have now started your project and entered your summary information.

Now you can move on to 'Step 2 – Develop Your Plan'.

Step 2 – Develop Your Plan

Once you've defined your project objectives, the next step is to plan how you will achieve them, how you will get there, by developing your project plan.

Before we start building the plan we need to look at some of the key things that make up a project plan. These are:

- Tasks

- Deliverables

- Milestones

- Resources

Tasks

Tasks are the basic building blocks of the project. In order to carry out a project you will need to carry out a sequence of individual but related tasks.

Deliverables

Deliverables not only allow you to measure completion, they also allow you to carry out quality assurance.

Deliverables (sometimes referred to as the Products of a project) are the things that the project will produce along the way. Typically reports, requirements, documents and acceptance certificates as well as the final product (whatever it is).

Milestones

Milestones are the points during the project when you can accurately measure your progress. They will typically be major events like approval to proceed or final acceptance.

Resources

Resources are the people and other things you will use on the project to carry out the tasks and produce the deliverables.

Your project plan will consist of the tasks needed to produce the deliverables and complete the project together with the resources you will use to perform them and the milestones you will use to measure your progress.

We will now look at these in a bit more detail.

Key Tasks and Deliverables

Any project consists of a number of tasks which need to be completed. It may consist of very few tasks or a very large number. Some tasks will be short tasks and others will take longer to complete. Some will be critical to the success of the project, while others may be less important.

The first step in producing your project plan is to begin listing the key tasks – the important ones, the ones that are critical to the success of the project. These will typically be related to a key deliverable. For example, if you were building a house, there would be a 'design' task which would have the 'house plans' as its deliverable.

If your project was to carry out a strategy study, the key tasks and deliverables would be something like:

Don't start typing in these tasks yet. We will do that in Chapter 3.

Key Tasks	Deliverables
Plan the study	Project Plan
Information gathering	Interview Notes
Produce draft requirements	Draft Requirements
Hold feedback sessions	Final Requirements
Develop recommendations	Recommendations
Perform risk analysis	Risk Log
Produce implementation plan	Implementation Plan
Report to management	Final Report

While you may well have many other tasks to carry out during your project and may have other deliverables you need to produce, these should represent the major ones.

If you are not sure about whether a task is a key task or not, play safe and include it. It is easy to remove something later if it is not required but missing something key could be fatal.

Project Milestones

Project milestones are the events that mark the completion of a major task or group of tasks in a project.

Typical milestones would be the decision to proceed, selection of a supplier, acceptance of a major piece of work and of course completion of the project. Milestones often mark the acceptance of a key deliverable.

Although a milestone will usually have zero duration, it is possible to set a milestone that is also a task (we will deal with this in a later topic).

A milestone normally has a zero duration. In other words, it marks a single point in time when something happens.

Once you have identified the key tasks and their deliverables in your project, you need to identify the major milestones. For a short project (such as our strategy study) there may be only one milestone – completion of the project.

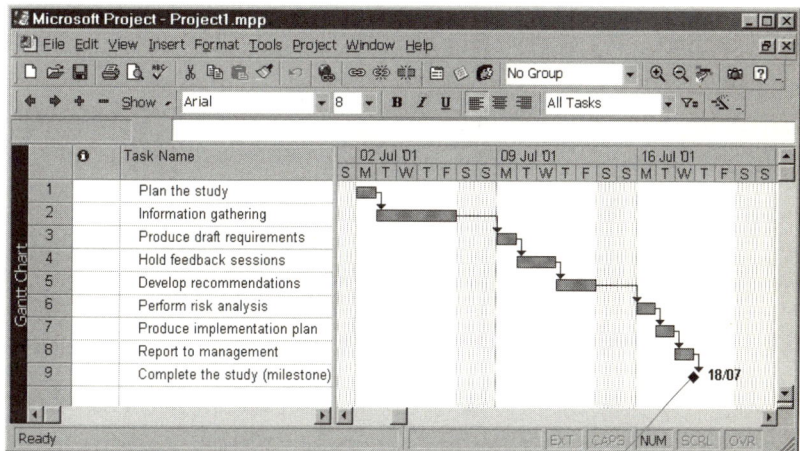

Project milestone

For a longer project there will be more, typically somewhere between three and eight.

Now look at your project key tasks and identify what your project milestones should be.

Resources

The key resources on most projects are people: the project manager (you) and anyone else you are going to use to do any work on the project.

You can also open Resource Sheet view by clicking View>Resource Sheet on the Menu Bar.

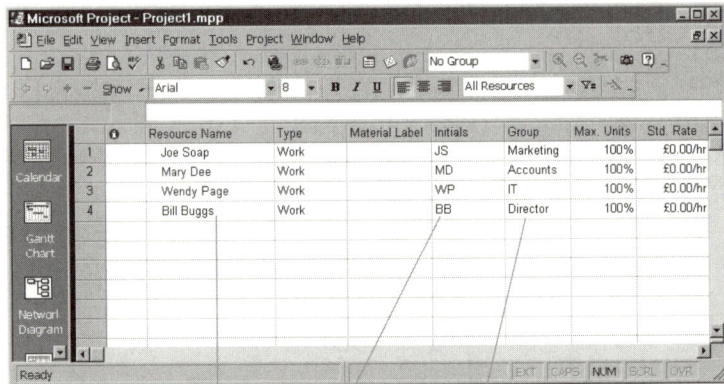

1 Click on Resource Sheet in the View Bar (it is near the bottom so you may need to scroll down to it). The Resource Sheet view opens.

		Resource Name	Type	Material Label	Initials	Group	Max. Units	Std. Rate
1		Joe Soap	Work		JS	Marketing	100%	£0.00/hr
2		Mary Dee	Work		MD	Accounts	100%	£0.00/hr
3		Wendy Page	Work		WP	IT	100%	£0.00/hr
4		Bill Buggs	Work		BB	Director	100%	£0.00/hr

2 Type in the names, initials and group for all the people who will be involved on your project. Leave the defaults in the other fields for now.

3 Then identify any other resources or facilities that your project will need and type them in after the people. Change their Type to Material:

To delete a single field use Ctrl+Delete. The delete key on its own deletes the whole record.

		Resource Name	Type	Material Label	Initials	Group	Max. Units
1		Joe Soap	Work		JS	Marketing	100%
2		Mary Dee	Work		MD	Accounts	100%
3		Wendy Page	Work		WP	IT	100%
4		Bill Buggs	Work		BB	Director	100%
5		Project Room	Material	Room		Facilities	
6		Personal Computer	Material	PC		Facilities	
7							

Don't worry about the other columns in the Resource Sheet; we will be dealing with them later.

The Full Monty

While the Gantt Chart produced by Project 2000 presents a good visual representation of the project plan, you may need to produce a more formal project document at the end of the planning exercise. This will be likely if it is a larger project or you require some sort of formal authority to proceed.

The following suggested content is based on a formal project plan and should be entered using your usual word processing software. It should have the following sections:

- *Background:* why the project is taking place.

- *The objectives of the project:* what it aims to achieve.

- *Any prerequisites:* things that must be available for the project to begin or continue.

- *External dependencies:* any outside agencies that may be involved as suppliers, partners or clients.

- *Planning assumptions:* anything that could impact the project.

- *Project Gantt Chart:* the summary level chart showing the main project stages.

- *Key deliverables:* the tangible things that the project will produce or deliver.

- *Budget:* the finance required to carry out the project in terms of real cost and nominal people cost (if relevant).

- *Resource requirements:* the key people and any other resources that the project will need to be successful. This should include the percentage of time they have to have available for the project.

This document forms the basis for agreement with your client, project sponsor, management, etc., and they will need to approve it for the project to continue. It is also good to show the project team what the project is about, and give them a chance to question and understand it.

One of the greatest problems in project management is not getting the key people or other resources you need when you need them.

Even if you are not carrying out the project for anyone else, it's still a good idea to produce an Outline Plan.

Step 3 – Carry It Out

One of the greatest mistakes made on projects is to jump straight in and get started. If you've skipped steps 1 and 2, go back and do them!

If you've been through Step 1 (Define Your Objectives) and Step 2 (Develop Your Plan), then you know where you're going and you have a plan for how you're going to get there. You will also have obtained any business approval you need to continue. You can now start carrying the project out.

There is often business pressure to skip these initial steps, particularly on smaller projects. It might sound good sense to just get stuck straight in and not waste time but it should be resisted. Carrying out a project without having clearly defined objectives and a proper plan is like building a new type of bridge from A to B, without knowing exactly where A is, and with the sure certainty that B will have moved by the time you get there.

Put simply, carrying out the project consists of allocating the necessary resources to the required tasks, tracking progress of the tasks until they are completed and measuring progress against your project milestones.

If only life were that simple the world would be a lovely place, but along comes Mr. Murphy:

Murphy's Law seems to apply doubly to IT projects and Channel Tunnels!

Murphy's 1st Law

Whatever *can* go wrong

will go wrong

So you also need to expect and to deal with problems. If you don't your project could rapidly get knocked off course. You can also benefit from the corollary to Murphy's First Law: 'If you plan on it going wrong it won't'.

Saving Your Project

The chances are that, sooner or later, everyone who works with a computer will lose a large amount of work through a power cut or some other problem outside of their control. I have even heard of some people (not me of course) who caused the problem themselves!

So whenever you are working on a computer, save your work regularly. Project 2000 is no exception to this rule. By saving your work you can try things out and always be able to get back to where you were. So save your project (and your sanity) by saving your work before (if you haven't already done so) and after making any major changes.

You can also click File>Save on the Menu Bar.

1 To save your file (replacing the previous version) simply click the Save button 🖫 on the Toolbar.

2 If you want to preserve the previous version of the project click File>Save As from the Menu Bar. Enter the directory where you want to save the file and new file name and click Save.

Project 2000 also contains an Auto Save feature in Tools>Options> Save>Auto Save from the Toolbar.

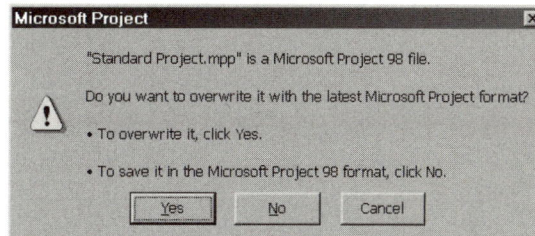

3 If you save a project that was originally created in Project 98 you will get a dialogue box asking if you want to save it in Project 98 (click No) or Project 2000 (click Yes) format.

Microsoft Project

"Standard Project.mpp" is a Microsoft Project 98 file.

Do you want to overwrite it with the latest Microsoft Project format?

* To overwrite it, click Yes.

* To save it in the Microsoft Project 98 format, click No.

[Yes]   [No]   [Cancel]

If you need to save your project files in Project 98 format for compatibility, you can set a default in Tools>Options> Save>Save files as.

4 If you save it in Project 98 format you will receive a further dialogue box warning you that some features may be lost on conversion. Click OK to continue with the Save.

Step 4 – Hand It Over

Once the project is completed, the project manager's role is finished. But some project managers have problems with this final step.

First you have to let go and let the people who will be responsible for the ongoing operation take over managing the process. They won't like it or feel comfortable if you are peering over their shoulders the whole time, so let them get on with it. You should have planned any required training and, once they are up to speed, they will be fine.

But, second, you cannot just dump the new process on them. As mentioned above, you should have planned any necessary training for them, but they will almost certainly have some problems adapting to new ways of doing things. What you must do is be available if they need you. This means scheduling some of your time to support the people doing the new process. This should only be for an initial, short critical period (usually around a month).

The hand over time is a great opportunity to finish off any outstanding paperwork or documentation. Tidy up the project files and back everything up.

The last scheduled task on the project should be to arrange and hold a post-implementation review. This is the time when you can go right back to the original objectives and see if they have been achieved or not. Was there anything that happened during the project that could not be dealt with or included in the project? If there was, should another project be initiated to deal with it?

As part of this review, the methods and tools used on the project should also be examined, and anything learnt should be noted for the benefit of future projects (your own, or those of anyone else in the organisation).

Last but not least, don't forget to thank everyone who helped you with the project, they will appreciate it.

Tasks and Milestones

Tasks represent the basic building blocks of a project and milestones are the reference points we use to measure progress. In this chapter we will use these to form the basic project plan.

Covers

Chapter Three

Project Tasks

Project tasks are the basic building blocks of a project plan. They represent the pieces of work that have to be done in order to carry out the project.

A project could be treated as just one very large task, but there would be two problems with this:

1.   It would be very difficult to estimate and schedule the effort required to carry it out. By breaking a project down into a number of smaller tasks, you will be able to estimate more accurately how long each will take and therefore how long the project will take in total.

2.   It would be very difficult to control it and measure progress until the project was complete. By splitting it into tasks you can track progress by the completion of individual tasks.

So split your project down into tasks that you can estimate, schedule and control.

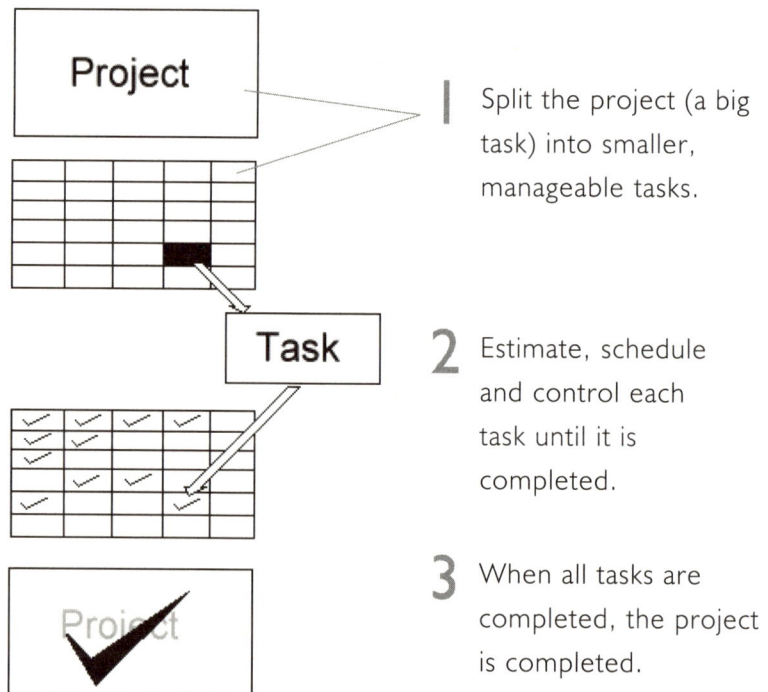

Project

1   Split the project (a big task) into smaller, manageable tasks.

Task

2   Estimate, schedule and control each task until it is completed.

3   When all tasks are completed, the project is completed.

Creating a Task

Although you will need to build up all the tasks involved in a project, it is very unlikely that you will be able to identify them all at the start. So to begin with you should just put in any key tasks that you have identified.

Tasks can be entered in any view that includes Task Name, but the Gantt Chart view (which is the default view) is the easiest one to use to build up your Task List.

1 Open your project file and switch to Gantt Chart view (if you are not already in it).

2 Click in the Task Name field.

3 Type 'Agree Project Objectives' and press Enter.

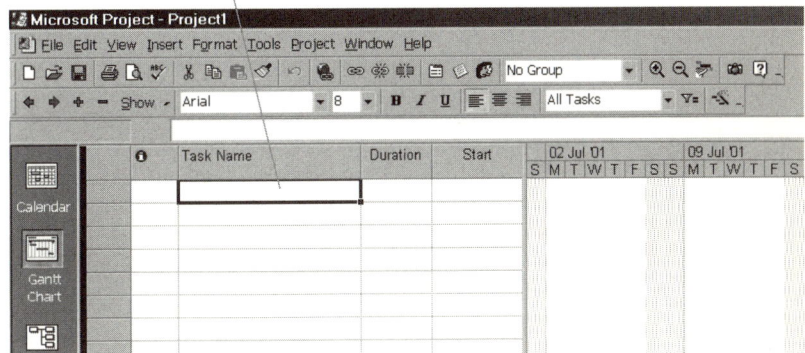

A Task ID (1) is automatically assigned and the default task duration of 1 day is allocated. The '?' after the duration indicates that it is an estimated duration at this stage.

4 Click the Save button on the Toolbar to save the project.

Task Duration

One of the main reasons for breaking a project down into tasks is to be able to estimate the amount of work effort required to complete it.

While it is easier to estimate the work effort involved in a small piece of work than a large piece you may still not know what's involved. So what can you base your estimate on?

The bigger the task the more unknown factors there will be, so increase your estimate to allow for this.

- *Experience* – if you've done something similar before, how long did it take?

- *Advice* – if you know someone who's done something similar, how long did it take them?

- *Guidelines* – does your organisation have any guidelines available for you to use?

- *Guess* – if none of the other options are available, your guess is probably as good as anyone else's!

Whatever method you use, it is worth getting someone else to check it. Two heads really are better than one when it comes to estimating.

All new tasks are automatically created with an estimated duration of 1 day by default. This is indicated by a '?' after the duration. Once you enter a duration the '?' is removed to show it is no longer an estimate. If, however, you are still not certain about the estimate you can enter any new value with a '?' to keep it as an estimate.

	ⓘ	Task Name	Duration	Start	02 Jul 01					
					S	M	T	W	T	F
1		Agree Project Objectives	1 day?	Mon 02/07/01						

This is a useful feature as you can easily spot the estimated durations and even select them using a filter (covered in a later topic).

You can change the task duration using the spin controls:

| Click on the Duration for Task 1 and use the spin controls to increase or reduce it.

	❶	Task Name	Duration	Start	02 Jul 01
					S M T W T F
1		Agree Project Objectives	2 days	Mon 02/07/01	

Notice that as soon as you change the duration the '?' disappears as it is no longer an estimated duration.

You can also change the duration by typing in the Duration field. If you just type a number it defaults to days – to use another unit you need to type it in after the number.

	❶	Task Name	Duration	Start	02 Jul 01
					S M T W T F
1		Agree Project Objectives	24 hrs	Mon 02/07/01	

working Time (8 hours working day)

2 To change the duration time unit type the number of Units followed by m (min), h (hrs), d (day), w (wk) or mo (month).

You can enter task duration as either Working Time (the default) or Elapsed Time. Working Time will be scheduled according to the Resources available to carry out the work, while Elapsed Time will be scheduled based on calendar days.

Notice above that 24 hours has been scheduled to take 3 working days (Monday to Wednesday) while below 24 hours' elapsed time will be scheduled as one day.

HOT TIP: For elapsed time type an 'e' in front of the type (em, eh, ed, ew or emo).

	❶	Task Name	Duration	Start	02 Jul 01
					S M T W T F
1		Agree Project Objectives	24 ehrs	Mon 02/07/01	

Adding Tasks

To add additional tasks at the end of an existing Task List, do the following:

1 Click on the first blank Task Name.

2 Type in 'Identify Project Team'. In Duration type '2' and press Enter.

	ⓘ	Task Name	Duration	Start	02 Jul '01 S M T W T F
1		Agree Project Objectives	1 day	Mon 02/07/01	

	ⓘ	Task Name	Duration	Start	02 Jul '01 S M T W T F
1		Agree Project Objectives	1 day	Mon 02/07/01	
2		Identify Project Team	2 days	Mon 02/07/01	

3 Now type in the following tasks and durations:

Produce Outline Project Plan	1d
Identify Business Case	2d
Analyse the Risks	1d

4 To insert a task into an existing Task List, click the Task Name for Task 2 (Identify Project Team) and select Insert>New Task from the Menu Bar.

You can also use the Insert key as a short cut to insert a task.

	ⓘ	Task Name	Duration	Start	02 Jul '01 S M T W T F
1		Agree Project Objectives	1 day	Mon 02/07/01	
2					
3		Identify Project Team	2 days	Mon 02/07/01	
4		Produce Outline Project Plan	1 day	Mon 02/07/01	
5		Identify Business Case	2 days	Mon 02/07/01	
6		Analyse the Risks	1 day	Mon 02/07/01	

If any task names do not fit into the field, double-click on the Task Name column header and select 'best fit'.

5 Type in 'Identify Stakeholders' and press Enter. Remember to save your project.

Task Dependencies

When you first identify your key tasks you should sequence them in the order that they will need to happen.

	❶	Task Name	Duration	Start	02 Jul '01
					S M T W T F S
1		Agree Project Objectives	1 day	Mon 02/07/01	
2		Identify Stakeholders	1 day	Mon 02/07/01	
3		Identify Project Team	2 days	Mon 02/07/01	
4		Produce Outline Project Plan	1 day	Mon 02/07/01	
5		Identify Business Case	2 days	Mon 02/07/01	
6		Analyse the Risks	1 day	Mon 02/07/01	

It looks from the above as though all the tasks will happen at the same time but that is not the way things usually happen in a project. Tasks are usually dependent on input from other tasks and other tasks are usually dependent on them.

Typically, Task 3 cannot begin until Task 2 has been completed...

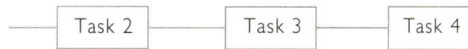

Task 2 —— Task 3 —— Task 4

...and once Task 3 has been completed, Task 4 can begin.

In Project 2000 you create these dependencies by linking tasks. Linking allows you to specify those circumstances where the start or finish of a task is dependent on the start or finish of another task.

The most common type of dependency or link is the finish-to-start dependency (as illustrated above) where the finish of Task 2 allows Task 3 to begin.

However there are three other types of link:

*   *Start-to-start:* Task 3 can start at the same time as Task 2.

*   *Finish-to-finish:* Task 3 must finish when Task 2 finishes.

*   *Start-to-finish:* when Task 2 starts Task 3 must finish.

But these are likely to be the exception rather than the rule.

Linking Tasks

Task dependencies are created by linking tasks.

The default dependency for linking tasks is a finish-to-start dependency and this will normally be the dependency you want for most tasks in a project. It is easiest to link all the tasks in a project in this way to start with and then make any changes to nonstandard links afterwards.

1 Select all tasks in the project by clicking the Task Name column header.

HOT TIP

You can also select tasks by dragging across the Task IDs or Task Names.

	ⓘ	Task Name	Duration	Start	02 Jul '01 S M T W T F S
1		Agree Project Objectives	1 day	Mon 02/07/01	
2		Identify Stakeholders	1 day	Mon 02/07/01	
3		Identify Project Team	2 days	Mon 02/07/01	
4		Produce Outline Project Plan	1 day	Mon 02/07/01	
5		Identify Business Case	2 days	Mon 02/07/01	
6		Analyse the Risks	1 day	Mon 02/07/01	

2 Click the Link Tasks button on the Toolbar: 🔗

	ⓘ	Task Name	Duration	Start	02 Jul '01 S M T W T F S	09 Jul '01 S M T W T F S
1		Agree Project Objectives	1 day	Mon 02/07/01		
2		Identify Stakeholders	1 day	Tue 03/07/01		
3		Identify Project Team	2 days	Wed 04/07/01		
4		Produce Outline Project Plan	1 day	Fri 06/07/01		
5		Identify Business Case	2 days	Mon 09/07/01		
6		Analyse the Risks	1 day	Wed 11/07/01		

The tasks are linked in a finish-to-start dependency.

You can select individual tasks to link by holding down Ctrl and clicking the individual Task Names or Task IDs.

HOT TIP

Get into the habit of saving your project after each topic or change. Then if anything goes wrong you can always go back to the saved version.

3 Save your project. It is a good idea to save your project after completing each topic or after making any changes unless something has gone wrong.

Unlinking Tasks

Once you have linked all the tasks in the project you may need to unlink some.

	ⓘ	Task Name	Duration	Start	02 Jul 01							09 Jul 01					
					S	M	T	W	T	F	S	S	M	T	W	T	F	S
1		Agree Project Objectives	1 day	Mon 02/07/01													
2		Identify Stakeholders	1 day	Tue 03/07/01													
3		Identify Project Team	2 days	Wed 04/07/01													
4		Produce Outline Project Plan	1 day	Fri 06/07/01													
5		Identify Business Case	2 days	Mon 09/07/01													
6		Analyse the Risks	1 day	Wed 11/07/01													

| Double-click the link between Task 2 (Identify Stakeholders) and Task 3 (Identify Project Team). The Task Dependency dialogue box opens.

2 Click Delete and the link is removed.

	ⓘ	Task Name	Duration	Start	02 Jul 01							09 Jul 01					
					S	M	T	W	T	F	S	S	M	T	W	T	F	S
1		Agree Project Objectives	1 day	Mon 02/07/01													
2		Identify Stakeholders	1 day	Tue 03/07/01													
3		Identify Project Team	2 days	Mon 02/07/01													
4		Produce Outline Project Plan	1 day	Wed 04/07/01													
5		Identify Business Case	2 days	Thu 05/07/01													
6		Analyse the Risks	1 day	Mon 09/07/01													

To unlink several tasks you can also drag across the tasks to select them.

You can also unlink tasks by holding down Ctrl, clicking on the tasks and then clicking the Unlink button on the Toolbar.

Changing Dependencies

Although the majority of tasks in a project will normally be in a finish-to-start dependency, you may need to change some to other types of dependencies:

1   Re-establish the dependency between Task 2 (Identify Stakeholders) and Task 3 (Identify Project Team) by selecting the tasks and clicking the Link Tasks button on the Toolbar.

2   Double-click the link between Task 5 (Identify Business Case) and Task 6 (Analyse the Risks) and the Task Dependency dialogue box opens.

3   Click the arrow to the right of Type.

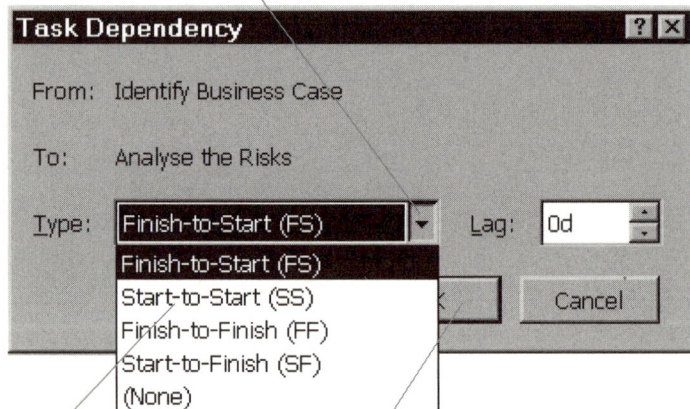

These four dependency types were defined in 'Task Dependencies'
on page 47.

Task Dependency

From: Identify Business Case

To: Analyse the Risks

Type: Finish-to-Start (FS)   Lag: 0d

- Finish-to-Start (FS)
- Start-to-Start (SS)
- Finish-to-Finish (FF)
- Start-to-Finish (SF)
- (None)

Cancel

4   Select Start-to-Start and click OK. The tasks are now rescheduled to start on the same day.

	ⓘ	Task Name	Duration	Start
1		Agree Project Objectives	1 day	Mon 02/07/01
2		Identify Stakeholders	1 day	Tue 03/07/01
3		Identify Project Team	2 days	Wed 04/07/01
4		Produce Outline Project Plan	1 day	Fri 06/07/01
5		Identify Business Case	2 days	Mon 09/07/01
6		Analyse the Risks	1 day	Mon 09/07/01

5 Save your project now before continuing with the remaining steps in this topic and do not save it at the end of the topic.

6 Double-click the link between Task 2 (Identify Stakeholders) and Task 3 (Identify Project Team) and when the Task Dependency dialogue box opens select 'Finish-to-Finish (FF)' as the dependency type and click OK.

	①	Task Name	Duration	Start	02 Jul '01 S M T W T F S
1		Agree Project Objectives	1 day	Mon 02/07/01	
2		Identify Stakeholders	1 day	Tue 03/07/01	
3		Identify Project Team	2 days	Mon 02/07/01	
4		Produce Outline Project Plan	1 day	Wed 04/07/01	
5		Identify Business Case	2 days	Thu 05/07/01	
6		Analyse the Risks	1 day	Thu 05/07/01	

Note what has happened to Task 3. As it is dependant on Task 2 with a finish-to-finish dependency it has to finish at the same time as Task 2. As it has 2 days' duration (work effort) Project 2000 has rescheduled it to start one day earlier than Task 2 so that it can still finish at the same time.

7 Now change the dependency between Task 4 (Produce Outline Project Plan) and Task 5 (Identify Business Case) to a 'Start-to-Finish (SF)' type and see what happens.

The use of start-to-finish dependencies is best avoided. It is easier to reverse the sequence of the tasks and use a standard finish-to-start dependency.

	①	Task Name	Duration	Start	02 Jul '01 S M T W T F S
1		Agree Project Objectives	1 day	Mon 02/07/01	
2		Identify Stakeholders	1 day	Tue 03/07/01	
3		Identify Project Team	2 days	Mon 02/07/01	
4		Produce Outline Project Plan	1 day	Wed 04/07/01	
5		Identify Business Case	2 days	Mon 02/07/01	
6		Analyse the Risks	1 day	Mon 02/07/01	

Project 2000 has now rescheduled Task 5 so that it finishes when Task 4 starts. This is a very unusual dependency type.

Moving a Task

If you need to move a task to a new position in the Task List, the easiest way is to drag and drop by selecting the ID of the task (or tasks) you want to move and then dragging them to their new position.

1 Click the Task ID for Task 4 (Produce Outline Project Plan) to select it. Make sure you release the mouse button.

Make sure you select the Task ID or you may only move the selected fields and not the whole task.

	0	Task Name	Duration	Start	02 Jul 01 S M T W T F S	09 Jul 01 S M T W T F S
1		Agree Project Objectives	1 day	Mon 02/07/01		
2		Identify Stakeholders	1 day	Tue 03/07/01		
3		Identify Project Team	2 days	Wed 04/07/01		
4		Produce Outline Project Plan	1 day	Fri 06/07/01		
5		Identify Business Case	2 days	Mon 09/07/01		
6		Analyse the Risks	1 day	Mon 09/07/01		

2 Now drag the task to after Task 6 (Analyse the Risks). Notice the insertion point marker as you drag.

5	Identify Business Case	2 days
6	Analyse the Risks	1 day

3 Release the mouse key. The task moves to its new position, its links are removed and the tasks are renumbered.

	0	Task Name	Duration	Start	02 Jul 01 S M T W T F S	09 Jul 01 S M T W T F S
1		Agree Project Objectives	1 day	Mon 02/07/01		
2		Identify Stakeholders	1 day	Tue 03/07/01		
3		Identify Project Team	2 days	Wed 04/07/01		
4		Identify Business Case	2 days	Fri 06/07/01		
5		Analyse the Risks	1 day	Fri 06/07/01		
6		Produce Outline Project Plan	1 day	Mon 02/07/01		

4 Select Tasks 4 and 6 and click the Link Tasks button on the Toolbar. Then do the same with Tasks 5 and 6 and finally save your project.

Deleting a Task

If you need to delete a task from the Task List, simply select it and delete it.

1 Select Task 2 (Identify Stakeholders) by clicking on its Task ID.

	❶	Task Name	Duration	Start
1		Agree Project Objectives	1 day	Mon 02/07/01
2		Identify Stakeholders	1 day	Tue 03/07/01
3		Identify Project Team	2 days	Wed 04/07/01
4		Identify Business Case	2 days	Fri 06/07/01
5		Analyse the Risks	1 day	Fri 06/07/01
6		Produce Outline Project Plan	1 day	Tue 10/07/01

You can also use the Delete key to delete one or more selected tasks.

2 Click Edit>Delete Task on the Menu Bar. The task is removed from the project:

	❶	Task Name	Duration	Start
1		Agree Project Objectives	1 day	Mon 02/07/01
2		Identify Project Team	2 days	Tue 03/07/01
3		Identify Business Case	2 days	Thu 05/07/01
4		Analyse the Risks	1 day	Thu 05/07/01
5		Produce Outline Project Plan	1 day	Mon 09/07/01

The Delete key deletes the whole task. If you want to delete the contents of one field use Shift+Delete.

3 If you delete the wrong task (or tasks) in error you can always reverse your last action. Click on the Undo button on the Toolbar.

Project 2000 only lets you undo the last action.

When you have used the Undo button it turns into the Redo button to allow you to cancel the Undo.

4 To redo whatever you have just corrected click the Redo button on the Toolbar.

The Redo button now turns back into the Undo button.

5 Click the Undo button again to restore the deleted task (Identify Stakeholders) again.

The Task Form

Task Entry view is one of the additional views that is available in Project 2000. You can use it to view, enter and edit details of individual tasks.

If the View Bar is not displayed you can get it back with View>View Bar on the Menu Bar.

1 Click the down arrow at the bottom of the View bar until More Views appears.

2 Click More Views.

3 Scroll down through the More Views list, select Task Entry and click Apply. The Task Form is displayed in the bottom half of the view.

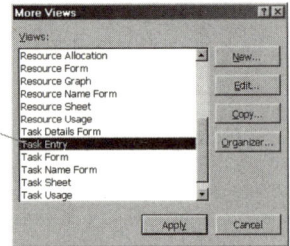

You can drag the split bar up and down to change the size of the top and bottom panes.

4 You can now view, enter and edit task details directly in the lower pane. You can also double-click the split bar to get back to Gantt Chart view.

Project Milestones

Project milestones are the key events that mark the progress of a project.

The simplest way of inserting a milestone is to enter a task with a zero duration.

1 Click on the blank Task Name below Task 6 (Produce Outline Project Plan).

2 Type 'Project Approval', press Tab, type '0' and press Enter. A milestone is inserted into the project plan.

3 Link Task 6 (Produce Outline Project Plan) and Task 7 (the milestone) by selecting them and clicking the Link Tasks button on the Toolbar.

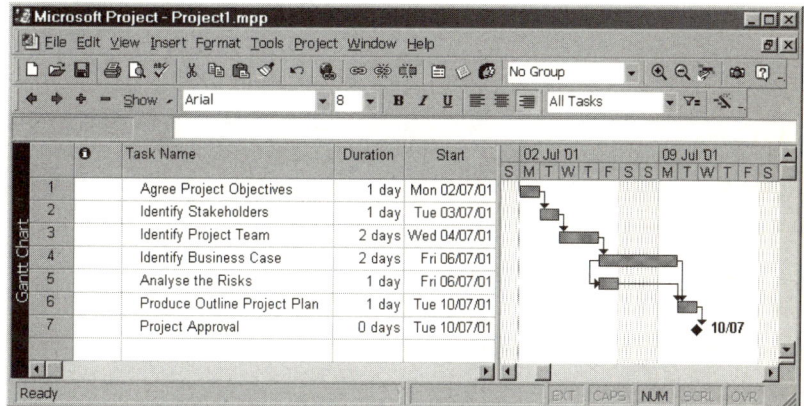

4 Click the Duration, type '5d' and double-click the task. The Task Information dialogue box opens.

5 Click the Advanced tab, click the Mark Task as Milestone checkbox and click OK. The task changes back to a milestone but the duration stays as 5 days.

Recurring Tasks

Any task that is repeated within a project is called a recurring task. It could be a regular project team meeting, a review with your project sponsor or production of a monthly management report.

1 To insert a recurring task, click in an empty Task Name field.

2 Click Insert>Recurring Task on the Menu Bar and the Recurring Task Information box appears.

3 Type 'Project Team Meeting';
type '1h';
select 'Weekly';
select 'Thursday';
and click OK.

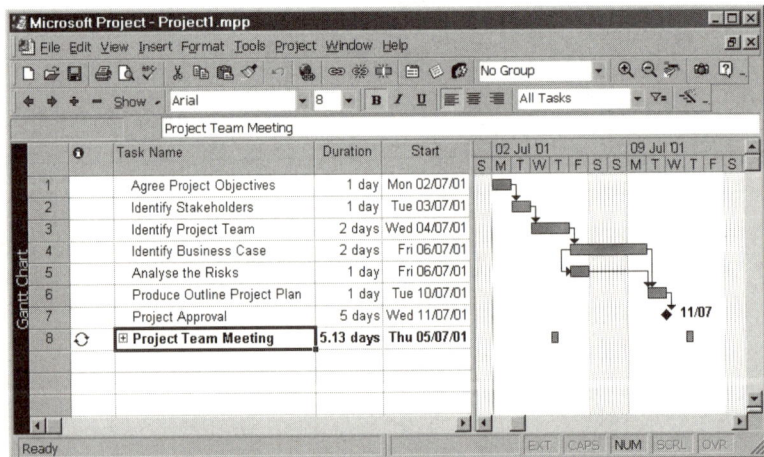

The recurring task is inserted. Click the '+' next to the Task Name to show the individual meetings. Note also the duration is 5.13 days (the two meetings and the time between them).

Adding Structure

In this chapter we begin to add some structure to the project by developing summary tasks and subtasks and using outlining.

Covers

Chapter Four

Project Structure

A simple project, like carrying out and presenting a strategy study, might consist of as little as a dozen tasks. A medium sized project, such as building a house or implementing a computer system, could run into over a hundred individual tasks. A very large project could run into thousands of tasks.

If you try to identify and plan for every individual task right from the outset you will almost certainly be doomed to failure. In the early stages of a project there will usually be a large number of unknown factors. These factors will only become known as the project progresses. To cope with this you need to break a project down into manageable chunks one level at a time. This is usually referred to as a Work Breakdown Structure and represented hierarchically:

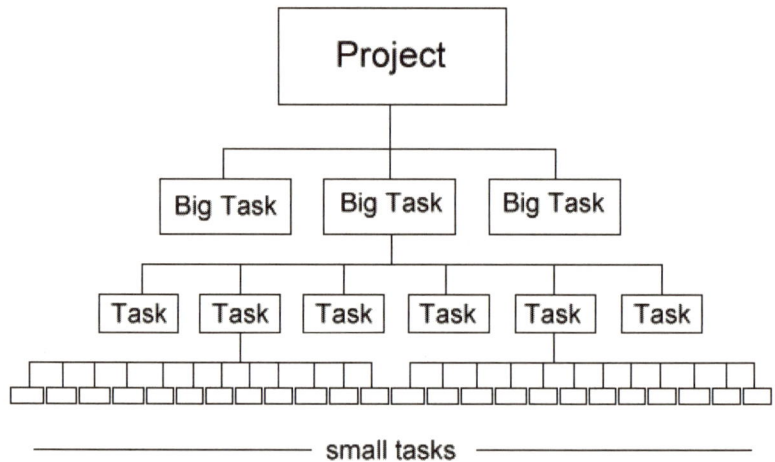

small tasks

I Break the project down into some discrete chunks (big tasks) with deliverables.

2 As you begin each big task, break it down into its individual tasks.

3 As you begin to work on each task, break it down into its individual subtasks (if relevant).

So when you first start a project you need to break it down into the first level major chunks (big tasks). Going back to our 4 step approach to carrying out a project we could use that as a basis for our big chunks. That would give us the following four steps as our first level big tasks:

1.   Define the objectives

2.   Plan the project

3.   Carry it out

4.   Hand it over

You would then start to identify the tasks required to carry out step 1 (defining the objectives) before worrying about the detailed tasks involved in step 2.

As you get towards the end of defining the objectives you would then start to identify and plan the detailed tasks in the next step (planning the project) and so on.

Working through the project in this manner means that there will be less unknown factors when you come to identify the tasks and estimate the effort involved in them.

In Project 2000, the process of structuring your project plan in this way is called Outlining. The Outlining buttons are on the Formatting Toolbar when in Gantt Chart view:

The Outlining buttons are also visible from within Task Sheet and Task Usage views.

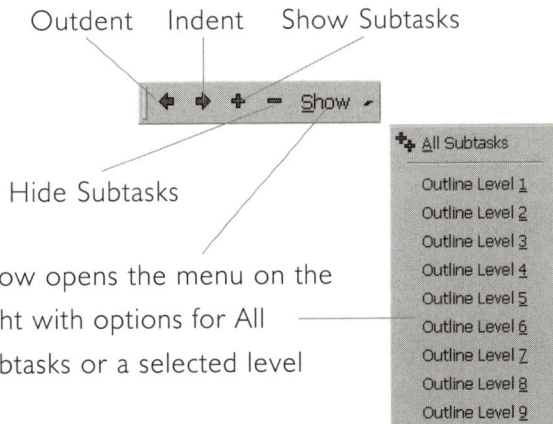

Outdent   Indent   Show Subtasks

Hide Subtasks

Show opens the menu on the right with options for All Subtasks or a selected level

All Subtasks

Outline Level 1
Outline Level 2
Outline Level 3
Outline Level 4
Outline Level 5
Outline Level 6
Outline Level 7
Outline Level 8
Outline Level 9

Summary Tasks

A summary task is created just like any other task, but its subtasks are indented.

1 Click Task 1 (Agree Project Objectives).

2 Click Insert>New Task on the Menu Bar (or press Insert).

3 Type the new Task Name 'Define the Objectives' and press Enter.

4 Select Tasks 2 to 8 by clicking and dragging their Task IDs and click the Indent button on the Toolbar.

	ⓘ	Task Name	Duration	Start	02 Jul 01 / 09 Jul 01 / 16 Jul 01
1		⊟ **Define the Objectives**	**12 days**	**Mon 02/07/01**	
2		Agree Project Objectives	1 day	Mon 02/07/01	
3		Identify Stakeholders	1 day	Tue 03/07/01	
4		Identify Project Team	2 days	Wed 04/07/01	
5		Identify Business Case	2 days	Fri 06/07/01	
6		Analyse the Risks	1 day	Fri 06/07/01	
7		Produce Outline Project P	1 day	Tue 10/07/01	
8		Project Approval	5 days	Wed 11/07/01	◆ 11/07
9	↻	⊞ **Project Team Meeting**	**5.13 days**	**Thu 05/07/01**	

These tasks have now become subtasks of Task 1 (Define the Objectives) and are indented. Task 1 has become a summary task and is now shown in bold. It also has a summary bar on the right hand side of the screen (note it shows the 5 days for the milestone).

5 Now hide the subtasks and insert the other three steps and durations as shown below.

	ⓘ	Task Name	Duration	Start	02 Jul 01 / 09 Jul 01 / 16 Jul 01
1		⊞ **Define the Objectives**	**12 days**	**Mon 02/07/01**	
9		Plan the Project	10 days	Mon 02/07/01	
10		Carry it Out	30 days	Mon 02/07/01	
11		Hand it Over	15 days	Mon 02/07/01	
12	↻	⊞ **Project Team Meeting**	**5.13 days**	**Thu 05/07/01**	

6 Save your project.

Task Rollup

Individual tasks are enabled by double-clicking the task name and setting the 'hide task bar' and 'roll up Gantt bar' features on the General tab.

The standard way that tasks roll up into summary tasks is as a solid summary bar (as shown on the Gantt Charts on the facing page). However the project meetings are also a summary task and clicking on the plus sign beside the summary task will display the individual meetings as separate tasks. But instead of a solid line the summary line shows the individual meetings. This is a default for recurring tasks but it can be enabled individually for each task and summary task. With Project 2000 you can now set it for the whole project.

1   Select Format>Layout from the menu bar. The layout dialogue box opens.

2   Select 'Always roll up Gantt bars' and 'Hide Rollup bars when summary expanded'.

3   Click OK. Nothing should look any different now.

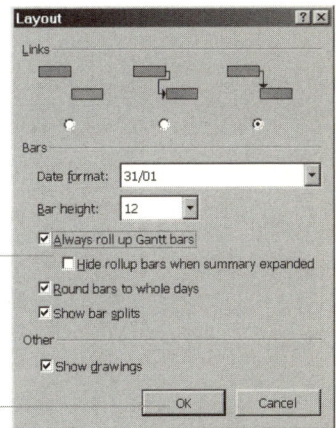

4   Now click the Show button on the menu bar and select 'Outline Level 1' and your project will be displayed at the top level with rolled up rather than summary Gantt bars:

	🛈	Task Name	Duration	Start	02 Jul 01							09 Jul 01					
					S	M	T	W	T	F	S	S	M	T	W	T	F	S
1		⊞ **Define the Objectives**	**12 days**	**Mon 02/07/01**													
9		Plan the Project	10 days	Mon 02/07/01													
10		Carry it Out	30 days	Mon 02/07/01													
11		Hand it Over	15 days	Mon 02/07/01													
12	↻	⊞ **Project Team Meeting**	**5.13 days**	**Thu 05/07/01**													

With this feature it is simple to change the way the whole project is displayed in summary views.

Changing the Time Scale

Once you begin to link the top level tasks on a project, they will go off the time scale in the right hand pane and you will not be able to see the whole project. However, this is easily remedied using the Zoom in and Zoom Out buttons on the Toolbar:

1 Link the new summary tasks by selecting Tasks 1 to 11 and clicking the Link Tasks button on the Toolbar.

2 Now use the Zoom In and Zoom Out buttons on the Toolbar until you have the whole project in view again.

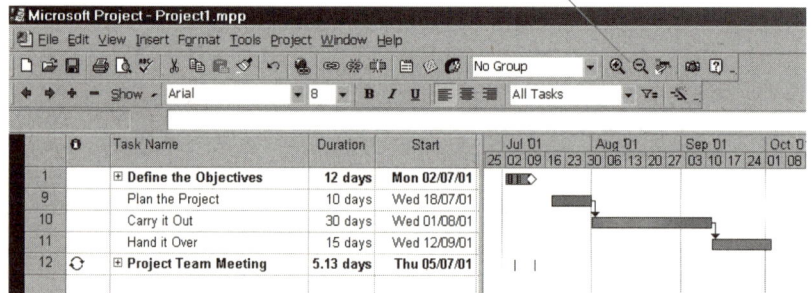

3 Now select Show All Subtasks from the Toolbar and use the Zoom In button to get back to the subtask details.

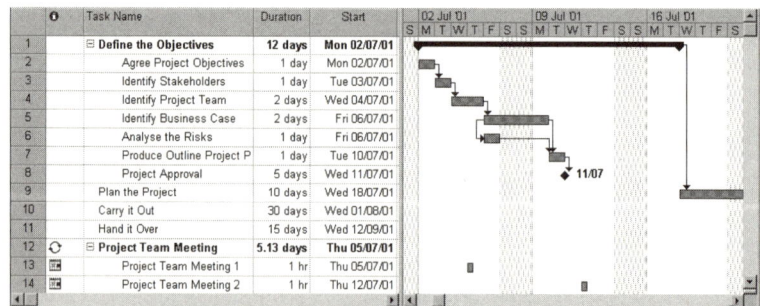

4 You may need to use the slider controls to bring the focus back to the required time period.

Project Stages

Conventionally in project management methodology, the first level summary tasks are referred to as project stages.

Project management methodology initially grew out of the construction industry and still retains some of that industry's terminology. In later years it has also been influenced by the software development industry which, interestingly, has a lot of similarities.

Using that influence, we can now build a little further on our four-step approach by expanding our second step (planning) into three separate stages:

• Determine what the business needs are.

• Define what we will need to do to achieve those needs.

• Work out how we are actually going to do it.

If this sounds a bit like 'overkill', keep an open mind for the time being. Hopefully you will begin to see why as we develop the process further. These six project stages are conventionally referred to as:

Some people refer to these project stages as project phases.

1. Initiation – to define the project objectives and team structure

2. Strategy – to determine the business needs and payback

3. Analysis – to define what we will need to do

4. Design – to work out how we will actually do it

5. Build – to carry it out, make it, buy it, manage it

6. Implement – to hand over the new process

The chief benefit of this method is that the major expense or effort usually occurs in the Build stage. At each of the preceding stages you are able to reappraise the potential investment and ensure that it will still be of benefit. If it becomes questionable, the project can be wound up while costs and effort expended are still relatively low.

Implementing a 6-Stage Approach

While the 6-stage approach may indeed be overkill for a strategy study or a smaller project, somewhere between 4 and 6 stages will usually fit most projects. Just use whichever stages are appropriate to your project.

1 Select Task 1 (Define the Objectives) and change the Task Name to 'Initiation'.

2 Select Task 9 (Plan the Project). Insert a new Task 9 'Strategy' and outdent it. Indent Task 10 (Plan the Project).

To insert more than one task, drag down the Task IDs to select the required number of tasks and press Insert.

3 Select Task 11 (Carry it Out). Insert and outdent three new tasks:

- Analysis
- Design
- Build

4 Select Task 14 (Carry it Out) and Indent it.

5 Select Task 15 (Hand it Over), insert a new task 'Implement' and outdent it, then indent Task 16 (Hand it Over).

6 Hide all subtasks and use Zoom Out on the Toolbar to get the whole project in view. Now delete Task 17 (Project Meetings) and it should look something like the following:

To switch back to summary bars use Format>Layout from the Menu bar.

	❶	Task Name	Duration	Start
1		⊞ Initiation	12 days	Mon 02/07/01
9		⊞ Strategy	10 days	Wed 18/07/01
11		Analysis Stage	1 day?	Mon 02/07/01
12		Design Stage	1 day?	Mon 02/07/01
13		⊞ Build Stage	30 days	Wed 01/08/01
15		⊞ Implement	15 days	Wed 12/09/01

Although you have now implemented the 6-stage approach it still needs a little more doing to it. We will finish it off in the next couple of sections.

Change Budgets — cushion for unknown's

When you first start a project you may be able to identify some of the key tasks but there will still be a lot of unknown factors, particularly in the later stages. To cope with this, and still be able to produce an outline schedule, you need to put in some sort of allowance, a change budget.

How Much?

How much change budget should you add to cope with these unknown factors? How long is a piece of string?

While there is no right answer to this question, there is a rule of thumb that seems to work for the author:

These amounts are based on medium sized projects — smaller projects should require less but larger projects will need more!

- add 100% to your initial estimate (yes, double it!)

- when you get to the end of the Strategy stage and estimate the remaining work on the project add 50%

- likewise at the end of the Analysis stage add 25%

- and finally at the end of the Design stage add 10%

What you will be doing through the project is identifying more tasks. As you identify these additional tasks you can reduce your change budget accordingly. Hopefully as you reach the end of each stage your change budget figure for that stage will be down to zero. It will have done its job.

Key Tasks

Before you put in your change budget figure it is a good idea to make sure you have identified any key tasks. Then you can put them in at the same time.

If the objective of the project was to select a new computer accounting package you would possibly have identified key tasks such as: Agree the Requirements; Select a Package; Purchase the Package; Install the Package; Train the Users; and Convert to the New Package. In the next topic we will put these tasks and a change budget into our project.

Adding a Change Budget

Your project should currently look something like the screen shot at the bottom of page 64 (if not enter the necessary tasks as described in 'Implementing a 6-Stage Approach').

1 Click the (show subtasks) plus sign beside Task 9 (Strategy), and change the name of Task 10 to 'Change Budget'.

2 Insert 4 new tasks in front of Task 12 (Design):

'Agree Requirements'	–	duration '5d'
'Select Package'	–	duration '5d'
'Purchase Package'	–	duration '2d'
'Change Budget'	–	duration '3d'

Link them and indent them.

3 Insert 'Change Budget' (10d) under Design and indent it. Insert 'Install Package' (5d) under Build, change 'Carry it Out' to 'Change Budget' (25d) and link them.
Under 'Implement' insert 'Train Users' (5d) and 'Convert to New Package' (5d), change 'Hand it Over' to 'Change Budget' (10d) and link and indent them if necessary.

4 Show all Subtasks and link the last subtask under each summary task (stage) to the first subtask in the next stage. Finally delete any stray or surplus links between stages.

	❶	Task Name	Duration	Start	
1		⊟ **Initiation**	**12 days**	**Mon 02/07/01**	
2		Agree Project Objectives	1 day	Mon 02/07/01	
3		Identify Stakeholders	1 day	Tue 03/07/01	
4		Identify Project Team	2 days	Wed 04/07/01	
5		Identify Business Case	2 days	Fri 06/07/01	
6		Analyse the Risks	1 day	Fri 06/07/01	
7		Produce Outline Project P	1 day	Tue 10/07/01	
8		Project Approval	5 days	Wed 11/07/01	
9		⊟ **Strategy**	**10 days**	**Wed 18/07/01**	
10		Change Budget	10 days	Wed 18/07/01	
11		⊟ **Analysis Stage**	**15 days**	**Wed 01/08/01**	
12		Agree Requirements	5 days	Wed 01/08/01	
13		Select package	5 days	Wed 08/08/01	
14		Purchase Package	2 days	Wed 15/08/01	
15		Change Budget	3 days	Fri 17/08/01	
16		⊟ **Design Stage**	**10 days**	**Wed 22/08/01**	
17		Change Budget	10 days	Wed 22/08/01	
18		⊟ **Build Stage**	**30 days**	**Wed 05/09/01**	
19		Install Package	5 days	Wed 05/09/01	

Breaking Tasks Down

Having inserted summary tasks (Stages) as the first level of the project work breakdown, their constituent tasks become the second level. If you then need to break those tasks down into further subtasks they become the third level on the project work breakdown.

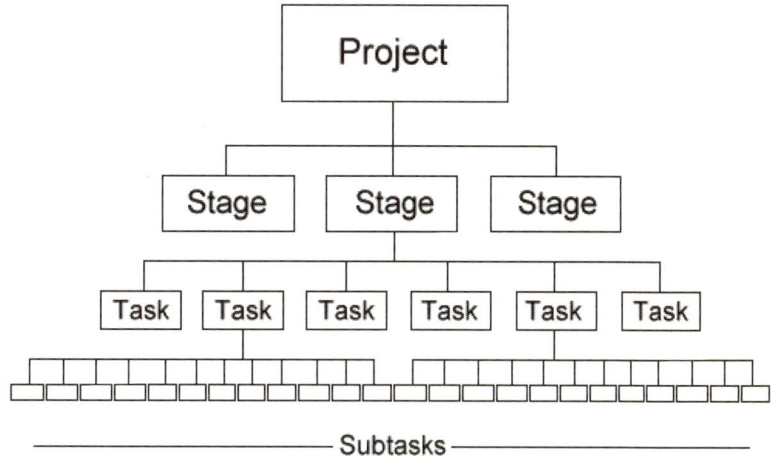

In project management methodology, these third level subtasks are usually called Activities.

So how big or small should a task be?

If you are to be able to estimate, schedule and control a task with any degree of accuracy, it needs to be small enough to allow you to do this. But it must be large enough to have some form of deliverable or product so that its completion can be confirmed. Finally, although more than one person may work on a task, only one person must be responsible for its completion.

Conventional wisdom is that a task should be between 1 and 10 days' effort (typically around 5 days). If it's bigger, then you should attempt to break it down into subtasks. If it's smaller, then see if you can combine it with some other task.

At the end of the day it's you, as the project manager, that should make the decisions, so these and any other guidelines are just that. If you want a 20 day task and it makes sense then have it, it's your project.

Outline Numbering

For a small project with a dozen or so tasks, the Task ID is probably a good enough way of keeping track of tasks. But as your project starts to build up you will want to be able to hide and show tasks and still keep track of where everything fits. Outline numbering allows you to achieve this.

1 Click Tools>Options on the Menu Bar. The Options dialogue box opens.

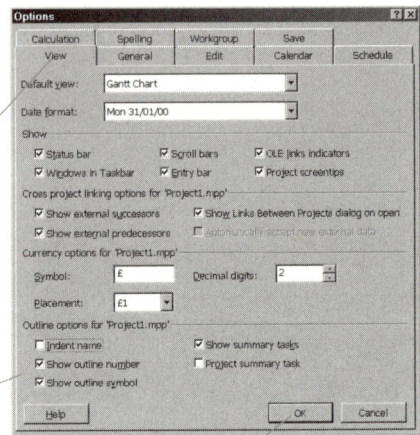

2 Make sure the View Tab is selected.

3 Check 'Show outline number' and un-check 'Indent name'.

4 Click OK.

5 Click Show Subtasks for Task 1 (Initiation).

If any task information is hidden from view, double-click the column header and select 'Best Fit'.

	ⓘ	Task Name	Duration	Start	02 Jul 01 S M T W T F S	09 Jul 01 S M T W T F S
1		⊟ **1 Initiation**	**12 days**	**Mon 02/07/01**		
2		1.1 Agree Project Objectives	1 day	Mon 02/07/01		
3		1.2 Identify Stakeholders	1 day	Tue 03/07/01		
4		1.3 Identify Project Team	2 days	Wed 04/07/01		
5		1.4 Identify Business Case	2 days	Fri 06/07/01		
6		1.5 Analyse the Risks	1 day	Fri 06/07/01		
7		1.6 Produce Outline Project Plan	1 day	Tue 10/07/01		
8		1.7 Project Approval	5 days	Wed 11/07/01		◆ 11/07
9		⊞ **2 Strategy**	**10 days**	**Wed 18/07/01**		
11		⊞ **3 Analysis Stage**	**15 days**	**Wed 01/08/01**		
16		⊞ **4 Design Stage**	**10 days**	**Wed 22/08/01**		
18		⊞ **5 Build Stage**	**30 days**	**Wed 05/09/01**		
21		⊞ **6 Implement**	**20 days**	**Wed 17/10/01**		

Your stages and tasks are now numbered in a structured format. Additional sub-subtasks below Task 1.4 will be numbered 1.4.1, 1.4.2 and so on.

Outline Codes

6

In addition to standard outline numbering, Project 2000 also lets you create your own custom outline codes which are held in the custom outline codes field. One or more tasks or resources (covered later) can then be assigned to the same outline code so they can be grouped together.

This feature could be useful if your project is part of a larger project or programme and you are required to use standard outline codes for your tasks.

1 To define a custom outline code select Tools > Customise > Fields from the Menu bar.

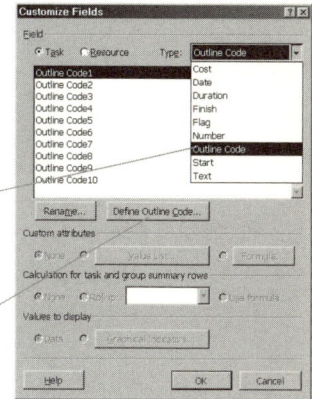

2 In the dialogue box select 'Outline Code' as the field type.

3 Then click the 'Define Outline Code' button. The definition box will open.

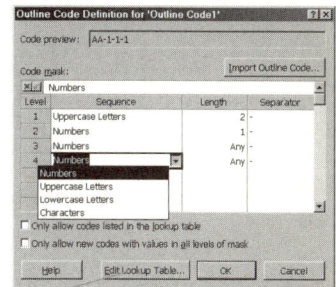

4 Now you can define each part of the code. In this case 2 upper case letters followed by three numbers with a dash separator.

5 Once you have defined your code structure, click on 'Edit Lookup Table'.

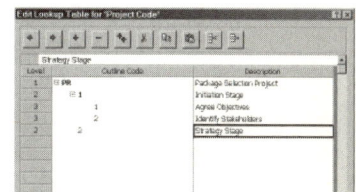

6 Then type in any look-up codes with their description. We will look at using and displaying these codes later.

Subtasks

Any task that is larger than 10 days' work effort will probably need to be split down into subtasks or the individual activities that make up the task. Even if a task is smaller than 10 days it may still be beneficial to split it down.

Activities

Third level subtasks are often referred to as Activities. They should be not less than half a day and not more than 5 days and should be carried out by one person. For example if you have two people assigned to a task, it should be split into (at least) two subtasks or activities, each of which is allocated to one person.

By allocating these bottom level activities to one person it becomes easier to estimate, schedule and control them: easier to estimate as you can involve the person who will be doing it; easier to schedule as it involves only one person's time; and easier to control as you have only one person to ask about progress.

	Open your project and show subtasks for Stage 2 (Strategy).
2	Insert the 9 new tasks with their durations as shown and delete the old 'Change Budget' task.
3	The new tasks should be linked; if not, link them.
4	You decide that 2 people will carry out the interviews so insert 2 new tasks after 2.1 (Carry out Interviews).

Task Name	Duration
⊞ 1 Initiation	12 days
⊟ 2 Strategy	15 days
2.1 Carry out interviews	4 days
2.2 Produce draft requirements	2 days
2.3 Feedback sessions	1 day
2.4 Consolidate results	1 day
2.5 Finalise requirements	1 day
2.6 Evolve other recommendatioı	1 day
2.7 Carry out risk analysis	2 days
2.8 Produce forward plan	1 day
2.9 Report to management	2 days
⊞ 3 Analysis	15 days
⊞ 4 Design	10 days
⊞ 5 Build	30 days
⊞ 6 Implement	20 days

⊟ 2 Strategy	15 days
2.1 Carry out interviews	4 days
2.2 Produce draft requirements	2 days

5 Type in the two new
subtasks and their durations
as shown (don't worry
about the outline numbers).

2 Strategy	15 days
2.1 Carry out interviews	4 days
2.2 Interview Managers	2 days
2.3 Interview Staff	2 days
2.4 Produce draft requirements	2 days

6 Select the two subtasks and indent them.

Task Name	Duration	Start	16 Jul '01	23 Jul '01	30 Jul '01
⊞ 1 Initiation	12 days	Mon 02/07/01			
⊟ 2 Strategy	15 days	Wed 18/07/01			
⊟ 2.1 Carry out interviews	4 days	Wed 18/07/01			
2.1.1 Interview Managers	2 days	Wed 18/07/01			
2.1.2 Interview Staff	2 days	Fri 20/07/01			
2.2 Produce draft requirements	2 days	Tue 24/07/01			
2.3 Feedback sessions	1 day	Thu 26/07/01			
2.4 Consolidate results	1 day	Fri 27/07/01			
2.5 Finalise requirements	1 day	Mon 30/07/01			
2.6 Evolve other recommendations	1 day	Tue 31/07/01			
2.7 Carry out risk analysis	2 days	Wed 01/08/01			
2.8 Produce forward plan	1 day	Fri 03/08/01			
2.9 Report to management	2 days	Mon 06/08/01			
⊞ 3 Analysis Stage	15 days	Wed 08/08/01			
⊞ 4 Design Stage	10 days	Wed 29/08/01			
⊞ 5 Build Stage	30 days	Wed 12/09/01			
⊞ 6 Implement	20 days	Wed 24/10/01			

Notice that Task 2.1 ('Carry out interviews') has now
become a summary task (with a '–' beside it) and the two
new subtasks are now numbered 2.1.1 and 2.1.2.

7 Hide the two new subtasks by clicking the '-' beside 2.1.

Task Name	Duration	Start	16 Jul '01	23 Jul '01	30 Jul '01
⊞ 1 Initiation	12 days	Mon 02/07/01			
⊟ 2 Strategy	15 days	Wed 18/07/01			
⊞ 2.1 Carry out interviews	4 days	Wed 18/07/01			
2.2 Produce draft requirements	2 days	Tue 24/07/01			
2.3 Feedback sessions	1 day	Thu 26/07/01			
2.4 Consolidate results	1 day	Fri 27/07/01			
2.5 Finalise requirements	1 day	Mon 30/07/01			
2.6 Evolve other recommendations	1 day	Tue 31/07/01			
2.7 Carry out risk analysis	2 days	Wed 01/08/01			
2.8 Produce forward plan	1 day	Fri 03/08/01			
2.9 Report to management	2 days	Mon 06/08/01			
⊞ 3 Analysis Stage	15 days	Wed 08/08/01			
⊞ 4 Design Stage	10 days	Wed 29/08/01			
⊞ 5 Build Stage	30 days	Wed 12/09/01			
⊞ 6 Implement	20 days	Wed 24/10/01			

Stages, Tasks and Activities

Summarising the content of this chapter, we have split a project down hierarchically into three levels: Stages, Tasks and Activities. This is the Work Breakdown Structure:

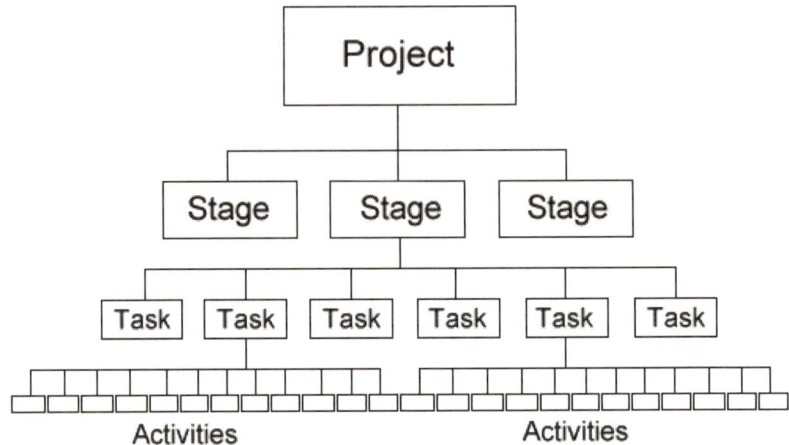

Stages

Stages are the first level summary tasks that define the structure of the project. The typical project will have around six of these main stages. In Project 2000 we set these up as summary tasks.

Tasks

Tasks are the basic building blocks of the project. Typically a task will be about 5 days' work effort and it will have some sort of deliverable.

Activities

Activities are the third level (detailed subtasks) of a project. Larger tasks will be split down into activities to enable the project manager to allocate, schedule and control the work. Activities will still have some sort of deliverable but will be carried out by one person.

By structuring your project this way and reflecting it in your project plan you will be able to manage and communicate your project in the most effective way.

More About Tasks

This chapter goes into tasks in a little more detail. It covers lag and lead times, task notes, setting deadline dates, the Critical Path and splitting and moving tasks.

Covers

Chapter Five

Lag Time and Lead Time

Up to now we have been linking tasks, mainly in a finish-to-start dependency, with the next task starting immediately after the preceding task finishes. However, there are times when you will want the tasks to overlap or have a gap between them.

Lag Time

Lag time is when there is a gap (or lag) between the finish of one task and the start of the next task.

Lead Time

Lead time is when there is an overlap, with the next task starting before the previous one has finished.

Use Zoom In and Out on the Toolbar to alter the time scale if necessary.

In Project 2000 these are both specified using the Lag field (a positive number being lag time and a negative number being lead time).

Note that we set the Project Approval (milestone) with a 5 day duration to allow for the approval decision although there was not 5 days work involved.

Task Name	Duration	Start			
			02 Jul 01	09 Jul 01	16 Jul 0
			S M T W T F S S	M T W T F S S	M T W
⊟ **1 Initiation**	**12 days**	**Mon 02/07/01**			
1.1 Agree Project Objectives	1 day	Mon 02/07/01			
1.2 Identify Stakeholders	1 day	Tue 03/07/01			
1.3 Identify Project Team	2 days	Wed 04/07/01			
1.4 Identify Business Case	2 days	Fri 06/07/01			
1.5 Analyse the Risks	1 day	Fri 06/07/01			
1.6 Produce Outline Project Plan	1 day	Tue 10/07/01			
1.7 Project Approval	5 days	Wed 11/07/01		◆ 11/07	
⊞ **2 Strategy**	**15 days**	**Wed 18/07/01**			

1 Show the subtasks in the Initiation stage of the project.

2 Double-click the link between 1.6 (Produce Outline Plan) and 1.7 (Project Approval). The Task Dependency dialogue box opens.

3 Change the Lag to 5d and click OK.

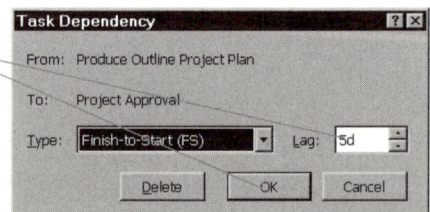

Task Dependency

From: Produce Outline Project Plan

To: Project Approval

Type: Finish-to-Start (FS)   Lag: 5d

Delete   OK   Cancel

4 Change the Duration of 1.7 (Project Approval) back to zero. The schedule now shows the correct milestone date with the 5 day lag:

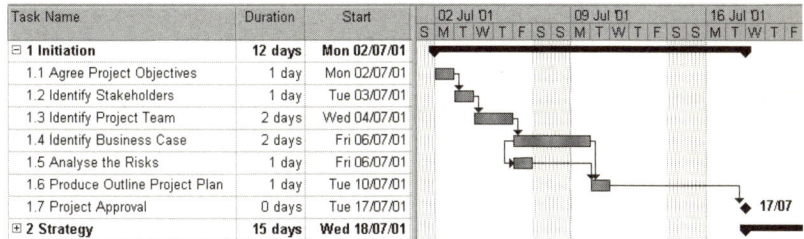

Task Name	Duration	Start	02 Jul 01	09 Jul 01	16 Jul 01
□ 1 Initiation	12 days	Mon 02/07/01			
1.1 Agree Project Objectives	1 day	Mon 02/07/01			
1.2 Identify Stakeholders	1 day	Tue 03/07/01			
1.3 Identify Project Team	2 days	Wed 04/07/01			
1.4 Identify Business Case	2 days	Fri 06/07/01			
1.5 Analyse the Risks	1 day	Fri 06/07/01			
1.6 Produce Outline Project Plan	1 day	Tue 10/07/01			
1.7 Project Approval	0 days	Tue 17/07/01			17/07
⊞ 2 Strategy	15 days	Wed 18/07/01			

Now let's look at putting in lead time:

1 Double-click the link between 1.3 (Identify Project Team) and 1.4 (Identify Business Case) to open the Task Dependency dialogue box.

You can also change the Lag time by double-clicking on the dependant task and altering Lag time in the Task Information dialogue box, Predecessors tab.

2 Click the down arrow spinner control to produce a Lag of '-1' and click OK.

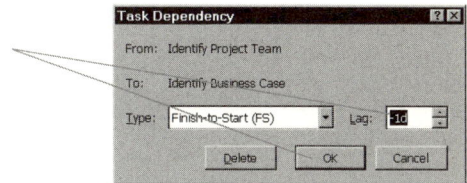

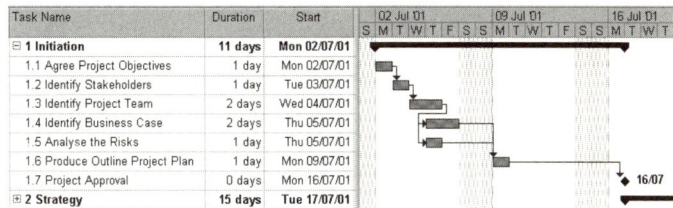

Task Dependency

From: Identify Project Team
To: Identify Business Case
Type: Finish-to-Start (FS)   Lag: -1d

Delete   OK   Cancel

Task Name	Duration	Start	02 Jul 01	09 Jul 01	16 Jul 01
□ 1 Initiation	11 days	Mon 02/07/01			
1.1 Agree Project Objectives	1 day	Mon 02/07/01			
1.2 Identify Stakeholders	1 day	Tue 03/07/01			
1.3 Identify Project Team	2 days	Wed 04/07/01			
1.4 Identify Business Case	2 days	Thu 05/07/01			
1.5 Analyse the Risks	1 day	Thu 05/07/01			
1.6 Produce Outline Project Plan	1 day	Mon 09/07/01			
1.7 Project Approval	0 days	Mon 16/07/01			16/07
⊞ 2 Strategy	15 days	Tue 17/07/01			

There is now a 1 day overlap between 1.3 (Identify Project Team) and 1.4 (Identify Business Case). We had already set the link between 1.4 and 1.5 (Analyse the Risk) as a start-to-start dependency so this task is now overlapped as well. We have also brought the project approval forward by one day.

Task Notes

You can add notes to a task in Gantt Chart view or any other Task view where the information box is displayed.

1 Open your project in Gantt Chart view.

2 Select Task 1.6 (Produce Outline Project Plan).

3 Click the Task Note button on the Toolbar. The Task Information dialogue box opens with the Notes tab selected.

4 Type in your note: 'Need to confirm report format for the Outline Plan' and click OK.

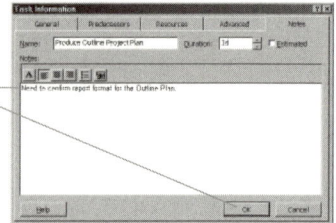

5 Pause the mouse pointer over the Note and the Note will pop-up on the screen:

Information Box   Task Note Button

Double-click the Note Indicator to edit the Note.

The Note Indicator (yellow note symbol) is displayed in the Information field for the task

Deadline Dates

Tasks can include a deadline date that allows an indicator to be displayed if a task is going to finish after its deadline. Deadline dates have little impact on the actual scheduling and should not be confused with task constraints (which we will see in a later topic) which can determine when a task will actually be scheduled.

Deadline dates are set on the Advanced tab of the Task Information dialogue box.

1 Open your project in Gantt Chart view and double-click on Task 1.2 (Identify Stakeholders). Select the Advanced tab on the Task Information dialogue box.

2 Click on the Deadline down arrow to get a calendar and select a date earlier than the current scheduled date. Then click OK.

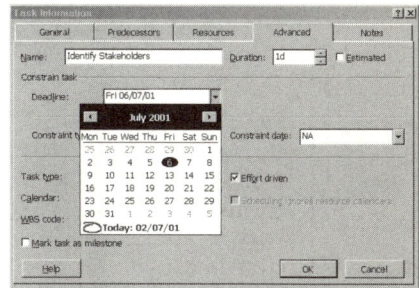

3 The task now has a warning indicator in the indicator column. Move your cursor over the indicator and the warning message will appear (as shown below).

Because Project 2000 will reschedule tasks as things change it is a good idea to set deadline dates on any relevant tasks.

ⓘ	Task Name	Duration	Start	02 Jul 01
				S M T W T F S
	⊟ **1 Initiation**	**11 days**	**Mon 02/07/01**	
	1.1 Agree Project Objectives	1 day	Mon 02/07/01	
⚠ ✚		1 day	Tue 03/07/01	
	This task finishes on Tue 03/07/01 which is later than its Deadline on Mon 02/07/01	2 days	Wed 04/07/01	
		2 days	Thu 05/07/01	
	1.5 Analyse the Risks	1 day	Thu 05/07/01	
📝	1.6 Produce Outline Project Plan	1 day	Mon 09/07/01	

Note that the Task bar on the Gantt Chart to the right now has a small arrow indicating the deadline.

Moving Around

As your project file starts to build up, you will not be able to get all the detailed information in one view at a time.

Scrollbars

You can use the scrollbars to scroll the view horizontally and vertically. The Gantt Chart view has one vertical scrollbar which moves the task information and time scale in step. It also has two horizontal scrollbars so that you can move through the task information independently of the time scale.

When you use the vertical scrollbar slider the task numbers are displayed in a pop-up box.

You can drag the divider between the Task list and Gantt chart to the left or right to get the desired amount of information on the screen.

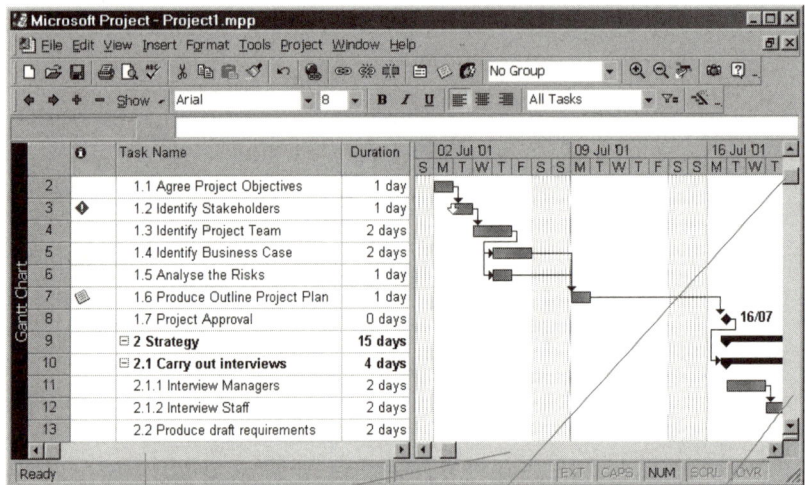

		0	Task Name	Duration
	2		1.1 Agree Project Objectives	1 day
	3	◆	1.2 Identify Stakeholders	1 day
	4		1.3 Identify Project Team	2 days
	5		1.4 Identify Business Case	2 days
	6		1.5 Analyse the Risks	1 day
	7		1.6 Produce Outline Project Plan	1 day
	8		1.7 Project Approval	0 days
	9		⊟ 2 Strategy	15 days
	10		⊟ 2.1 Carry out interviews	4 days
	11		2.1.1 Interview Managers	2 days
	12		2.1.2 Interview Staff	2 days
	13		2.2 Produce draft requirements	2 days

Horizontal Scrollbars   Vertical Slider   Vertical Scrollbar

Go To Selected Task

You can also use the Go To Selected Task button on the Toolbar to bring any task into view in the time scale:

1 Click on Task 15 (Consolidate Results).

2 Click the Go To Selected Task button on the Toolbar. (The time scale scrolls to the selected task.)

78 | Project 2000 in easy steps

The Critical Path

The Critical Path is the term given to the sequence of tasks that are critical to the duration of the project. A Critical Task is one that, if delayed or lengthened, will directly affect the project finish date.

The following diagram represents a simple project consisting of four tasks. Tasks A, B and D are each of two days' duration, while Task C is of one day's duration. Tasks B and C are both dependant on Task A with finish-to-start relationships. Task D is dependant on both Tasks B and C, again with finish-to-start relationships. Assuming no lag time the total duration of the project is six days.

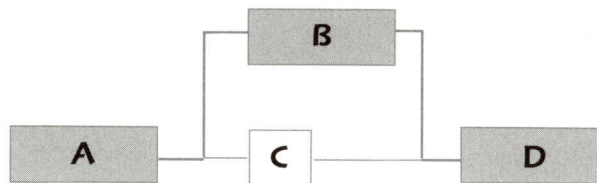

Even if task C were to slip by one day it would still not impact the completion of Task D and therefore the project would still be completed in six days. Task C is therefore not deemed to be a Critical Task.

On the other hand, if any of tasks A, B or D were to slip by one day the project would take seven days to complete and these tasks are therefore deemed to be Critical Tasks.

The Critical Path is the path through the project that links all of the Critical Tasks. In the diagram above the Critical Path (shown as a heavier line and shaded boxes) consists of Task A, the link between Task A and Task B, Task B, the link between Task B and Task D, and finally Task D.

In Project 2000 the Critical Path is calculated by the Gantt Chart Wizard which is covered in the next topic.

Gantt Chart Wizard

The Critical Path through the project is calculated by the Gantt Chart Wizard. The default is that it will display the Critical Path and Critical Tasks in red and non-Critical Tasks and path in blue.

1   In Gantt Chart view, click the Gantt Chart Wizard button. The Wizard Step 1 dialogue box appears.

2   Click Next and the Step 2 dialogue appears.

In case you are worried about the missing steps, they allow you to change the standard defaults for the way the Gantt Chart is displayed. To see what they are select 'Custom Gantt Chart' at Step 2.

3   Select 'Critical Path' and click Next. The Step 9 (yes there's no mistake) dialogue box appears.

4   Select 'Resources and Dates' and click Next. The Step 13 dialogue box appears.

5   Select 'Yes, please' to display links and click Next. The Step 14 dialogue box appears.

6   Click the 'Format It' button. The Step 15 (finished) dialogue box appears.

7   Click the 'Exit Wizard' button. The Gantt Chart is now re-formatted.

Non-critical Task (blue)   Critical Path (red)

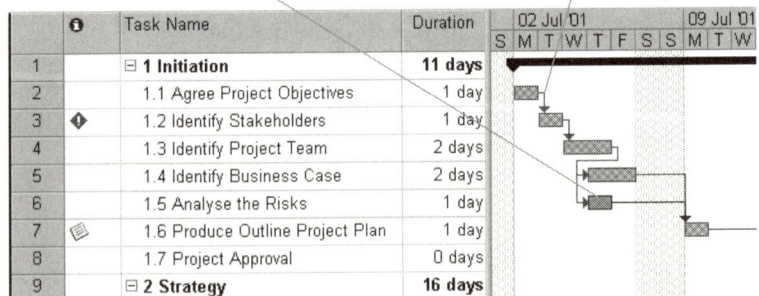

	❶	Task Name	Duration	02 Jul 01	09 Jul 01
				S M T W T F S	S M T W
1		⊟ 1 Initiation	11 days		
2		1.1 Agree Project Objectives	1 day		
3	◆	1.2 Identify Stakeholders	1 day		
4		1.3 Identify Project Team	2 days		
5		1.4 Identify Business Case	2 days		
6		1.5 Analyse the Risks	1 day		
7	🗎	1.6 Produce Outline Project Plan	1 day		
8		1.7 Project Approval	0 days		
9		⊟ 2 Strategy	16 days		

Splitting Tasks

Normally a task will be worked on from start to finish. However, a task can be split if it needs to be interrupted and finished at a later date.

We have a Task 2.1.1 'Interview Managers'. If some of the managers were going to be away at a conference, you would need to reschedule part of this task for their return.

1 Select Task 11 (Interview Managers).

2 Click the Split Task button on the Toolbar. A pop-up asks you to select the split point.

	❶	Task Name	Duration	16 Jul 01
				S M T W T F S
9		⊟ **2 Strategy**	**15 days**	
10		⊟ **2.1 Carry out interviews**	**4 days**	
11		2.1.1 Interview Managers	2 days	
12				
13		Split Task:		
14		Start:	Wed 18/07/01	
15		Click the mouse to insert a split on the task.		

3 Position the pointer in the middle of the Gantt bar for the task and click. The task is split and a gap of one day is opened.

4 Drag the right hand half of the task along to the next Monday and release it.

	❶	Task Name	Duration	16 Jul 01	23 Jul 01
				S M T W T F S	S M T W T F S
9		⊟ **2 Strategy**	**18 days**		
10		⊟ **2.1 Carry out interviews**	**7 days**		
11		2.1.1 Interview Managers	2 days		
12		2.1.2 Interview Staff	2 days		
13		2.2 Produce draft requirements	2 days		

The task is now split with a dotted line showing the link between the two halves and the project duration extended.

Moving Linked Tasks

When you split the task in the previous topic you left a gap in the Gantt chart. It would make sense to bring the following task (Interview Staff) forward to fill this gap:

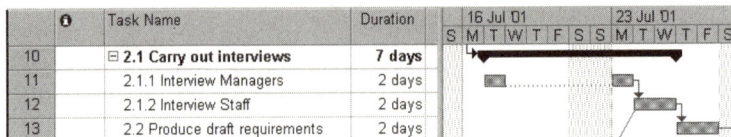

	❶	Task Name	Duration	16 Jul '01 ... 23 Jul '01
10		⊟ 2.1 Carry out interviews	7 days	
11		2.1.1 Interview Managers	2 days	
12		2.1.2 Interview Staff	2 days	
13		2.2 Produce draft requirements	2 days	

1 Position the mouse pointer over the Interview Staff Gantt Chart bar. The pointer changes into a Move pointer: ✛

2 Drag the Task bar back to start after the first half of Interview Managers and release the key. A Planning Wizard appears telling you that the link cannot be honoured.

3 Select 'Remove the link...' and click OK. The tasks are unlinked and a new Critical Path is established.

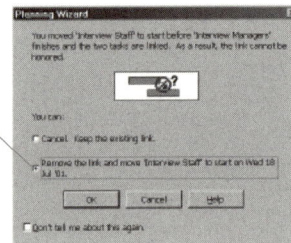

A calendar note has been added to the task with a 'Start No Earlier Than' constraint as we forced it to this date by moving it. We will deal with constraints in a later topic.

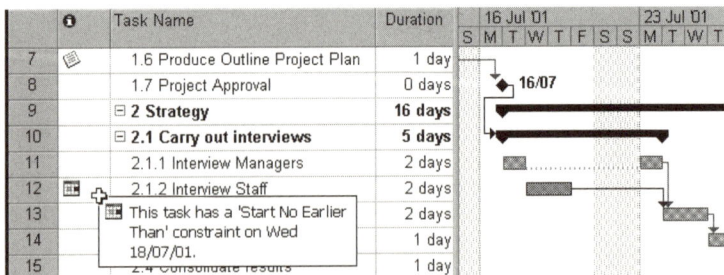

4 Select 2.1.1 (Interview Managers) and 2.2 (Produce Draft Requirements) and click the Link Tasks button to re-establish the Critical Path. Note that a calendar icon has been placed in the information column. Position your cursor over it.

	❶	Task Name	Duration	16 Jul '01 ... 23 Jul '01
7		1.6 Produce Outline Project Plan	1 day	
8		1.7 Project Approval	0 days	16/07
9		⊟ 2 Strategy	16 days	
10		⊟ 2.1 Carry out interviews	5 days	
11		2.1.1 Interview Managers	2 days	
12		2.1.2 Interview Staff	2 days	
13		This task has a 'Start No Earlier Than' constraint on Wed 18/07/01.	2 days	
14			1 day	
15		2.4 Consolidate results	1 day	

Resources

Up to now we have been looking at planning a project. This chapter introduces organising a project and working with project resources.

Covers

Chapter Six

Organising a Project

Organisation is a key area for a project manager. If you are not organised you will quickly lose track of what's happening on your project. The things you will need to organise on your project are the resources that you are going to use in order to complete the tasks and produce the deliverables.

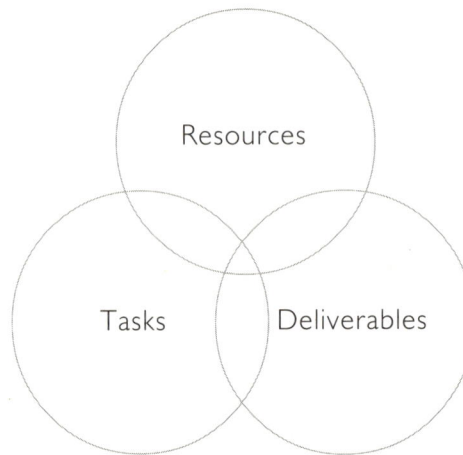

Resources

Resources represent the people and facilities that you will use on your project. As you have seen in the previous chapters, you can produce and schedule a project without assigning resources to it. In fact, if you are going to be doing all the work on a project yourself, you may not even bother to allocate resources (yourself) to the project. On the other hand if you are going to have other (non-project) work to deal with or if you are going to need other people and things on your project then you will be able to organise the project much better if you allocate resources.

In Project 2000 you can store lots of information about the resources you will use on your project. Anything from availability to costs.

Fortunately, setting up resources and allocating them is very straightforward with Project 2000.

Project Stakeholders

The major resources on most projects will be people: the people who will be involved in the project; the people who will do the work. But there are also other people with a vested interest in the outcome of a project: people who will be impacted by it in some way. They could include your management, staff impacted by any changes and even your suppliers and customers. The generic term for all these people and groups is 'project stakeholders'.

It is a good idea to start out by listing all your project stakeholders. You may not need to enter them all as resources but you should certainly keep the list available as you will probably need to think about communicating with them about the project from time to time.

So produce a list of your project stakeholders. Make sure you include:

- Your project sponsor or project board (whoever you report to about the project).

- Your project team (the people who will be working with you on completing the tasks).

- Any other people in the business who will be affected by the outcome of the project.

- Customers and suppliers (both internal and external) who will be affected by the outcome of the project.

- Anyone else who could be affected by the project.

When you have identified them all, think about the impact that they could have on your project. If they could have an impact in any way then you need to make sure you communicate what's happening on the project to them.

Remember that no-one likes being kept in the dark and you want them all on your side – not against you when the chips are down!

Allocating Resources

People who are assigned to a project are usually assigned on some form of temporary basis. That is, they will be working on your project for a set period of time. They will usually have other jobs and they may even have to keep on doing those other jobs for part of the time while they are also working on your project.

If you have someone allocated to your project for less than 50% of their time, you may find it hard to get them to prioritise project work over their other work.

If you have a person allocated to your project on anything less than a full-time basis you will need to take account of their other work commitments. This will sometimes be on the basis of their being allocated to the project for a certain number of days per week or month. Other times it might be on the basis of their being allocated to the project for a percentage of their time (typically 50–80%).

It will be very important to get a firm agreement on any part-time allocations up front, as you may need to fight for key resources at critical times. These are the sort of factors that need to be recorded as part of your project planning document.

The question you must ask yourself is how many days will a person work per week or per month on your project? If you know exactly when they will be available day-by-day then you can work that way. If not, you need some sort of rule to work to. Something that allows for them to be on holiday, on training courses, off sick, attending company meetings, etc. As a rule of thumb you could use the following:

In practice we have found that it works out at around 180 days on average as there will always be other things that can eat into peoples' time.

There are 52 weeks in a year, less 5 weeks' annual leave, less 2 weeks' public holidays, less 1 week's sickness, less 2 weeks' training, less 2 weeks for other work-related things that will impact them. That leaves 40 weeks at 5 days a week or 200 days. If they are allocated to your project full-time you will get less than 4 days' work a week from them. If they are not allocated full-time you will get proportionally less. Allocate people and schedule them on this basis (rather than 5 days a week) and you will not get caught out in the resource trap.

The Resource Sheet

If you worked through chapter 2 you will already have put in some resources. If not you can add them in now or at the end of this topic (they are all shown on the lower figure).

You can also open it using View>Resource Sheet from the Menu Bar.

1 Open your project file and click Resource Sheet on the View Bar. The Resource Sheet opens.

	ⓘ	Resource Name	Type	Material Label	Initials	Group	Max. Units
1		Joe Soap	Work		JS	Marketing	100%
2		Mary Dee	Work		MD	Accounts	100%
3		Wendy Page	Work		WP	IT	100%
4		Bill Buggs	Work		BB	Director	100%
5		Project Room	Material	Room		Facilities	
6		Personal Computer	Material	PC		Facilities	

2 Click in the first Resource Name field, press Insert and type your project manager's name. Click in Initials and enter them. Click in Group, enter 'Proj Mgr' and press Enter. (Don't worry about the other columns for now, just accept the defaults.) Your resources should look like the following:

The Group field does not have to be used for Department or Group. It can be used for anything you like.

	ⓘ	Resource Name	Type	Material Label	Initials	Group
1		Prudence Project	Work		PP	Proj Mgr
2		Joe Soap	Work		JS	Marketing
3		Mary Dee	Work		MD	Accounts
4		Wendy Page	Work		WP	IT
5		Bill Buggs	Work		BB	Director
6		Project Room	Material	Room		Facilities
7		Personal Computer	Material	PC		Facilities

Once your project is under way you may need to add, amend or even delete resources but it can all be done from this handy Resource Sheet view.

Resource Information

In addition to the Resource Sheet view there is also a Resource Information dialogue box.

1 Select one of the Resource Names (Joe Soap) on the Resource Sheet and click the Resource Information button on the Toolbar. The Resource Information dialogue box opens.

2 On the General Tab you can input and edit information for this resource. Make the following changes:

- Available from: 01/09/01
- Units: 50% (click the down arrow)
- Code: A209
- Email: jsoap@bigco.com
- Workgroup: Email

3 Click on the Details button to add more information (such as contact details) and update your e-mail address book. When you are happy with the entry click OK.

Material Resources

In addition to people, you can also put in other resources or facilities you will be using on your project:

1 Open your project in Resource Sheet view and add in the two additional Material resources (resources 8 and 9).

For consumable materials (e.g. paint) the Material Label should specify the units of charge (e.g. litres).

	❶	Resource Name	Type	Material Label	Initials	Group	Max. Units
1		Prudence Project	Work		PP	Proj Mgr	100%
2		Joe Soap	Work		JS	Marketing	0%
3		Mary Dee	Work		MD	Accounts	100%
4		Wendy Page	Work		WP	IT	100%
5		Bill Buggs	Work		BB	Director	100%
6		Project Room	Material	Room		Facilities	
7		Personal Computer	Material	PC		Facilities	
8		Board Room	Material	Room		Facilities	
9		Overhead Projector	Material	OHP		Facilities	

2 Now select one of the material resources and click on the Resource Information button on the Toolbar. Notice on the General tab that all the people-related fields are deselected.

3 Select the Costs tab and the following will be displayed.

Costs are covered in more detail in the next chapter.

There are two cost fields 'Standard Rate' and 'Per Use Cost'. Standard Rate is used where you will be charged for the duration of the use (e.g. a project room for the duration of the project), while Per Use Cost would apply to occasional use of a facility (e.g. a boardroom for presentations).

Resource Notes

In the same way as you can attach notes to tasks, you can attach notes to a resource:

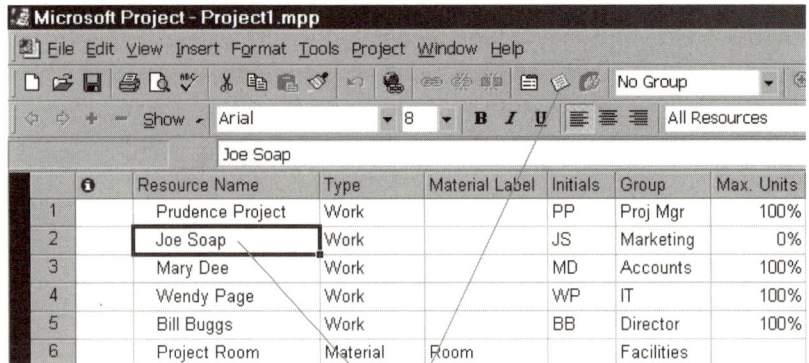

On the Resource Sheet select a Resource Name and click the Resource Notes button on the Toolbar. The Resource Information dialogue box opens at the Notes tab.

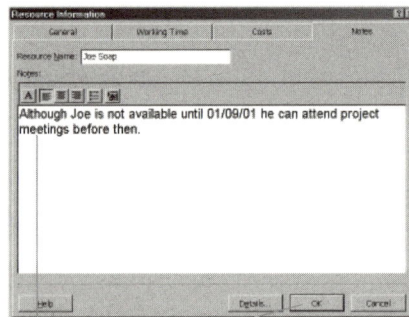

2 Type in your note and click OK. The Resource Sheet now shows a Note in the Information field:

If you hold the mouse pointer over the Note it will pop-up on the screen.

Assigning Resources

The process of allocating a resource to a task is called assigning.

1 Open your project in Gantt Chart view, select Task 2 (Agree Project Objectives) and click the Assign Resources button on the Toolbar.

2 The Assign Resources dialogue box appears. Select your project manager's name and click Assign.

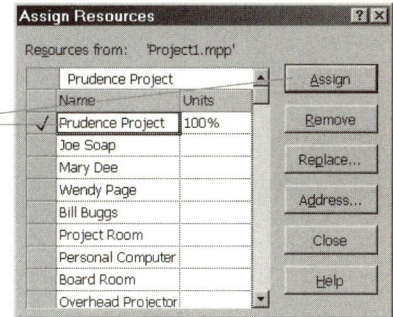

3 Select Task 3 (Identify Stakeholders) and assign your project manager.

4 Select Task 4 (Identify Project Team), select 'Bill Buggs', assign him to the task and click Close.

The Gantt Chart now shows the assignments. Note that these assignments were made at Units of 100% (the whole resource being allocated to the task).

Multiple Resources

So far we have just assigned a single resource to each task (which is in fact the best way of controlling a project). However, sometimes you need to assign two or more people or other resources to a task.

1 Select Task 4 (Identify Project Team) and click the Assign Resources button.

2 In the Assign Resources dialogue box, click your project manager and click Assign.

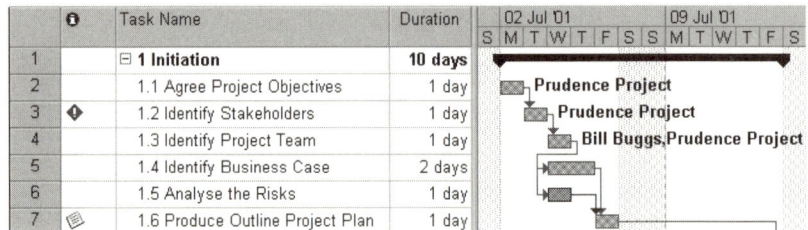

	❶	Task Name	Duration	02 Jul '01	09 Jul '01
				S M T W T F S	S M T W T F S
1		⊟ **1 Initiation**	**10 days**		
2		1.1 Agree Project Objectives	1 day	Prudence Project	
3	◆	1.2 Identify Stakeholders	1 day	Prudence Project	
4		1.3 Identify Project Team	1 day	Bill Buggs,Prudence Project	
5		1.4 Identify Business Case	2 days		
6		1.5 Analyse the Risks	1 day		
7	📋	1.6 Produce Outline Project Plan	1 day		

This is the standard method of scheduling but there are other options we shall look at in a later topic.

Note that both resources are now allocated to the task and that the duration has reduced to 1 day (2 resources x 1 day duration = 2 days work).

3 In order to keep the duration at 2 days, we can change the Units entry to 50% by clicking the down arrow in the Units field.

The task is rescheduled back to 2 days

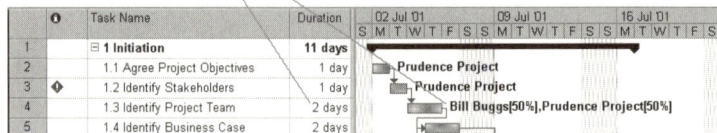

Assign Resources ? ✕

Resources from: 'Project1.mpp'

	50%		
	Name	Units	
✓	Prudence Project	50%	
	Joe Soap		
	Mary Dee		
	Wendy Page		
✓	Bill Buggs	50%	
	Project Room		
	Personal Computer		
	Board Room		
	Overhead Projector		

Assign
Remove
Replace...
Address...
Close
Help

	❶	Task Name	Duration	02 Jul '01	09 Jul '01	16 Jul '01
				S M T W T F S	S M T W T F S	S M T W T F S
1		⊟ **1 Initiation**	**11 days**			
2		1.1 Agree Project Objectives	1 day	Prudence Project		
3	◆	1.2 Identify Stakeholders	1 day	Prudence Project		
4		1.3 Identify Project Team	2 days	Bill Buggs[50%],Prudence Project[50%]		
5		1.4 Identify Business Case	2 days			

At the moment Task 5 (Identify Business Case) is scheduled to start one day before the end of Task 4 (we put in a 1-day lead time in an earlier topic) but we haven't yet assigned anyone to the task. We'll now see what happens when we do:

4 Select Task 5 (and click the Assign Resources button if you had closed it) and assign your project manager to the task.

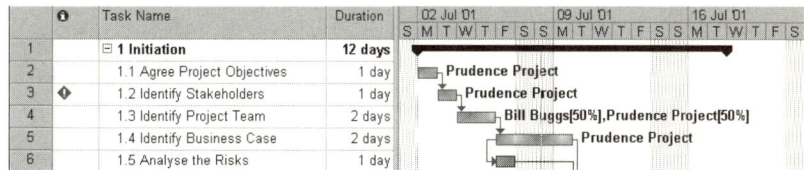

	❶	Task Name	Duration	02 Jul 01 S M T W T F S	09 Jul 01 S M T W T F S	16 Jul 01 S M T W T F S
1		⊟ 1 Initiation	12 days			
2		1.1 Agree Project Objectives	1 day	Prudence Project		
3	◆	1.2 Identify Stakeholders	1 day	Prudence Project		
4		1.3 Identify Project Team	2 days	Bill Buggs[50%],Prudence Project[50%]		
5		1.4 Identify Business Case	2 days	Prudence Project		
6		1.5 Analyse the Risks	1 day			

Note that as the project manager is already assigned to the previous task (Identify the Project Team) for the first day of Task 5, Project 2000 reschedules Task 5 to begin on the day following the completion of Task 4 (despite the fact that we put in a 1 day lead time). This is because a resource cannot be in two places or doing two tasks (if fully allocated to them) at once.

5 Now assign Bill Buggs to Task 5 as well but keep the Units for both at 100%. The task duration is reduced to 1 day

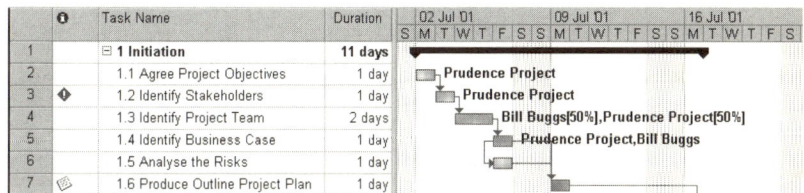

	❶	Task Name	Duration	02 Jul 01 S M T W T F S	09 Jul 01 S M T W T F S	16 Jul 01 S M T W T F S
1		⊟ 1 Initiation	11 days			
2		1.1 Agree Project Objectives	1 day	Prudence Project		
3	◆	1.2 Identify Stakeholders	1 day	Prudence Project		
4		1.3 Identify Project Team	2 days	Bill Buggs[50%],Prudence Project[50%]		
5		1.4 Identify Business Case	1 day	Prudence Project,Bill Buggs		
6		1.5 Analyse the Risks	1 day			
7		1.6 Produce Outline Project Plan	1 day			

Following on from what we have been doing in this topic you should be able to see from the above illustration that if we now allocate either our project manager or Bill Buggs to the next task (Analyse the Risks) it will no longer be able to take place at the same time as Task 5 (even though we have put it in a start-to-start relationship with it).

Multiple Tasks

As well as being able to assign multiple resources to a single task, you can also assign resources to multiple tasks:

1 Select Task 6 (Analyse the Risks).

2 Hold down Ctrl and select Task 7 (Produce Outline project Plan) and Task 11 (Interview Managers).

3 Click the Assign Resources button on the Toolbar, select your project manager, click Assign and then Close.

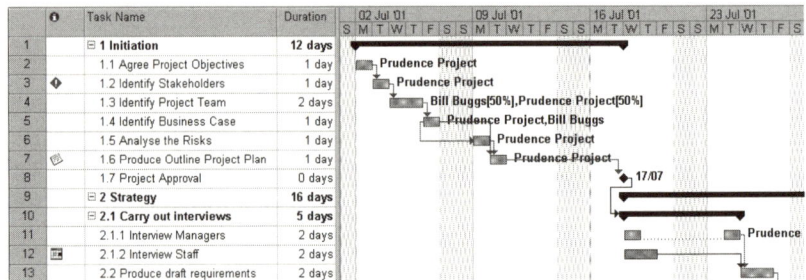

	0	Task Name	Duration	02 Jul 01	09 Jul 01	16 Jul 01	23 Jul 01
1		⊟ 1 Initiation	12 days				
2		1.1 Agree Project Objectives	1 day	Prudence Project			
3	◆	1.2 Identify Stakeholders	1 day	Prudence Project			
4		1.3 Identify Project Team	2 days	Bill Buggs[50%],Prudence Project[50%]			
5		1.4 Identify Business Case	1 day	Prudence Project,Bill Buggs			
6		1.5 Analyse the Risks	1 day		Prudence Project		
7	✐	1.6 Produce Outline Project Plan	1 day		Prudence Project		
8		1.7 Project Approval	0 days			◆ 17/07	
9		⊟ 2 Strategy	16 days				
10		⊟ 2.1 Carry out interviews	5 days				
11		2.1.1 Interview Managers	2 days				Prudence
12	▥	2.1.2 Interview Staff	2 days				
13		2.2 Produce draft requirements	2 days				

The three tasks have now been rescheduled so that each one starts following the end of the previous task. Note that where we put in a delay by splitting Task 11 (Interview Managers) so that the second day started on the following Monday, Project 2000 has put this back to Tuesday (keeping the split constant). We can now correct this:

4 Simply place your cursor on the second section of the Task bar (the cursor will change to four arrows showing the task can be moved) and drag it back to the previous day.

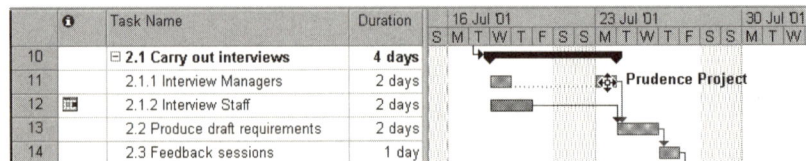

	0	Task Name	Duration	16 Jul 01	23 Jul 01	30 Jul 01
10		⊟ 2.1 Carry out interviews	4 days			
11		2.1.1 Interview Managers	2 days		Prudence Project	
12	▥	2.1.2 Interview Staff	2 days			
13		2.2 Produce draft requirements	2 days			
14		2.3 Feedback sessions	1 day			

Project Costs

In this chapter we look at adding costs to resources and tasks in order to build up the project budget and confirm (or reappraise) the business case for the project.

Covers

Chapter Seven

Project Costs

Be very careful with your preliminary costs or they can become cast in stone.

One of the first questions a project manager gets asked is 'How much is all this going to cost?' and it's usually only moments after being 'given' the project in the first place!

No-one can be expected to produce a reliable cost estimate until they have a full grasp of the business requirements. This will only be available a couple of stages into the project. So, anything produced before then should be clearly identified as a preliminary estimate and issued with a corresponding 'health warning'.

Use Your Experts

Get your Accounts department to run your budgets for you if you can. It's what they're good at.

The people within a business who are best able to produce accurate cost estimates will normally reside in a Finance or Accounts section. Using them should not only save the project manager a lot of time, but should also ensure the accuracy of the figures. Some organisations will allocate a finance person to each project as a project accountant. If not here is a guide to developing project costs.

Costing

Take the internal people work effort (including any change budget) and cost it up (Project 2000 will do this for you). Then add any other internal or external resource or material costs (again Project 2000 will help with this). Then add any recurring costs (the ongoing costs of operating the new product). We will now look at each of these in turn:

Internal People Costs

If the business operates on a cost centre principle, or charges clients for peoples' time, it may already have internal charging rates for its people. If not, they can be calculated.

Take the average annual salary for each grade of person working on the project (that way we don't have to know our colleagues' actual salaries!). Double it (to allow for premises and all the other costs of running the business) and divide it by 180 (as explained in 'Allocating Resources' on page 86) to get a daily internal cost. It is probably a good idea to check this figure with your finance people to see if they can come up with anything better.

This cost can be used to cost up the time each team member will spend on the project to give the total internal people cost.

External People Costs

External people working on a project will be charging for their time in some way. It may be a fixed cost for providing a service or it may be on a daily or hourly rate. Whatever it is can be used as the external people cost.

Other Project Costs

These could include costs for a project office, furniture, computers, telephones, secretarial services, etc. There may be software costs (such as Project 2000) and there may be a need to include travel or other appropriate costs.

Capital Costs

The costs of computers or other equipment, software packages or development, operating systems or database costs will normally be treated as capital (although the business may lease them). The relevant suppliers (or potential suppliers) should provide all of these costs for you. Your business will probably have a standard way of treating capital dependant on whether they lease or purchase and how they depreciate it.

Revenue Operating Costs

Finally the ongoing or operating costs of the new product need to be determined for its expected lifetime. The annual charge for the capital costs will be determined by the business (see above). The other operating costs will need to be calculated. These could include staff (additional people to operate the new product), annual maintenance or support costs for hardware (computer or otherwise), annual support or maintenance for software, operating systems, database licences and any other recurring costs in the project.

This may not be a complete list, there may be other costs that you should account for.

Costs in Project 2000

Having looked at some general considerations about costing in the previous topic, let us now look at how Project 2000 can help. Essentially Project 2000 covers all the (one-off) project costs but not the ongoing operating costs of any solution.

Project 2000 treats costs under two headings: Resource Costs (costs related to the people and material resources you will use on the project) and Fixed Costs (which are not related to resource usage).

Resource Costs

Once you have identified all the stages, tasks and activities for a project, you will have estimated the work effort required to carry out the project. This should include the appropriate element of change budget (to deal with the unknown) based on where you are in the project. By adding resource costs for all the internal people who will be working on the project, Project 2000 will calculate all the people-related costs for you.

Then you need to identify any external people costs such as consultants, auditors, etc. and feed those in as well.

Fixed Costs

Once you have the internal and external resource costs, you then need to identify any internal non-staff costs such as the use of facilities, rooms, computer usage, etc.

Finally you will need to identify any other external capital or revenue costs such as software package purchase, software development, equipment purchase or lease costs and any other items of external expenditure.

All these costs can be input into Project 2000 as Resource Costs or Fixed Costs on an appropriate task.

We will now work through each of these types of costs and how they are treated in Project 2000 in the remaining topics in this chapter.

Resource Costs

Costs can be applied to resources or tasks. Typically you will use resource costs for people on the project. Costs are shown as an hourly rate which can represent their hourly pay rate or salary plus overheads or whatever standards you use for costing in your business.

The easiest way to allocate costs to resources is through the Resource Sheet.

1 Open the Resource Sheet by clicking View>Resource Sheet on the Menu Bar.

If any resources are listed in red they are over allocated. This is dealt with in Chapter 10.

	Resource Name	Type	Material Label	Initials	Group	Max. Units	Std. Rate	Ovt. Rate
1	**Prudence Project**	**Work**		PP	**Proj Mgr**	100%	£20.00/hr	£30.00/hr
2	Joe Soap	Work		JS	Marketing	0%	£25.00/hr	£37.50/hr
3	Mary Dee	Work		MD	Accounts	100%	£15.00/hr	£22.50/hr
4	Wendy Page	Work		WP	IT	100%	£20.00/hr	£30.00/hr
5	Bill Buggs	Work		BB	Director	100%	£40.00/hr	£40.00/hr
6	Project Room	Material	Room		Facilities		£0.00	
7	Personal Computer	Material	PC		Facilities		£0.00	
8	Board Room	Material	Room		Facilities		£0.00	
9	Overhead Projector	Material	OHP		Facilities		£0.00	

2 Enter the applicable standard hourly rates and overtime rates for the resources.

Although the default rate is hourly, you can input annual salary by adding a '/y' after it.

	Resource Name	Type	Material Label	Initials	Group	Max. Units	Std. Rate	Ovt. Rate	Cost/Use
1	**Prudence Project**	**Work**		PP	**Proj Mgr**	100%	£20.00/hr	£30.00/hr	£0.00
2	Joe Soap	Work		JS	Marketing	0%	£25.00/hr	£37.50/hr	£0.00
3	Mary Dee	Work		MD	Accounts	100%	£15.00/hr	£22.50/hr	£0.00
4	Wendy Page	Work		WP	IT	100%	£20.00/hr	£30.00/hr	£0.00
5	Bill Buggs	Work		BB	Director	100%	£40.00/hr	£40.00/hr	£0.00
6	Project Room	Material	Room		Facilities		£0.00		£0.00
7	Personal Computer	Material	PC		Facilities		£0.00		£0.00
8	Board Room	Material	Room		Facilities		£0.00		£0.00
9	Overhead Projector	Material	OHP		Facilities		£0.00		£10.00

3 Where a resource has a cost per use (such as the hire of an overhead projector) enter it in the Cost/Use field.

It is possible for a resource to have both an hourly rate and a per use cost, the per use cost being charged once each time it is used and the hourly rate charged for the task duration.

Fixed Costs

Fixed costs are used where a task has a cost associated with it rather than the cost being associated with the resource. For example, Task 24 (Purchase Package) will be the purchase cost of selected software.

Project 2000 has adaptive menus, so if you don't see the item you want either click on the expand item (double chevron) or allow your pointer to hover over the menu and it will expand.

1 Select the Gantt Chart view then click View>Table: Entry> Cost on the Menu Bar. The cost columns will be moved into the view replacing the entry columns.

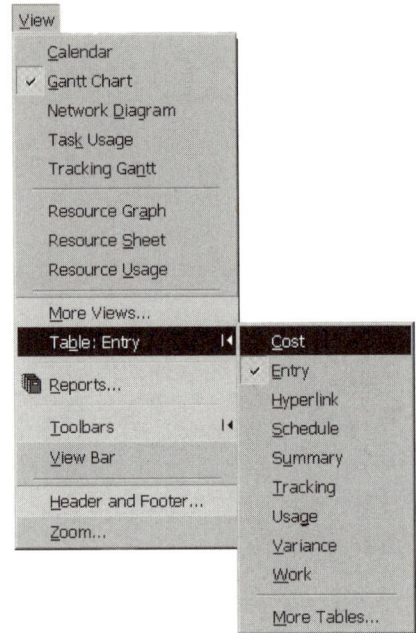

View	
	Calendar
✓	Gantt Chart
	Network Diagram
	Task Usage
	Tracking Gantt
	Resource Graph
	Resource Sheet
	Resource Usage
	More Views...
	Table: Entry ◄
	Reports...
	Toolbars ◄
	View Bar
	Header and Footer...
	Zoom...

Table: Entry submenu:
- Cost
- ✓ Entry
- Hyperlink
- Schedule
- Summary
- Tracking
- Usage
- Variance
- Work
- More Tables...

2 Type in the estimated fixed cost for the relevant task.

	Task Name	Fixed Cost	Fixed Cost Accrual	Total Cost	20 Aug '01 S M T W T F S	27 Aug '01 S M T W T F S
1	⊞ 1 Initiation	£0.00	Prorated	£1,600.00		
9	⊞ 2 Strategy	£0.00	Prorated	£320.00		
21	⊟ 3 Analysis Stage	£0.00	Prorated	£20,320.00		
22	3.1 Agree Requirements	£0.00	Prorated	£0.00		
23	3.2 Select package	£0.00	Prorated	£0.00		
24	3.3 Purchase Package	£20,000.00	Prorated	£20,320.00		Prudence Project
25	3.4 Change Budget	£0.00	Prorated	£0.00		
26	⊞ 4 Design Stage	£0.00	Prorated	£0.00		
28	⊞ 5 Build Stage	£0.00	Prorated	£0.00		
31	⊞ 6 Implement	£0.00	Prorated	£0.00		

3 Select the task and assign the project manager to it. The total cost now includes the fixed cost and the resource cost.

Variable Resource Costs

During the life of a project it is quite possible that resource costs could change. For example, someone may receive a salary increase for doing such a good job on the project. Any cost changes should be entered through the Resource Information dialogue box.

1 In Resource Sheet view, select the project manager and click the Resource Information button on the Toolbar.

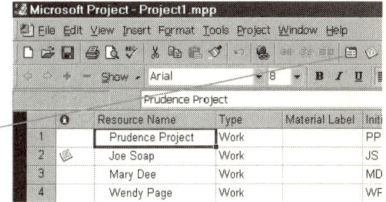

2 Click the Costs tab, click in the next Effective Date field and click the down arrow to get the calendar.

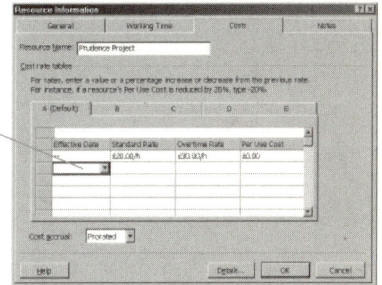

3 Select 1 September.

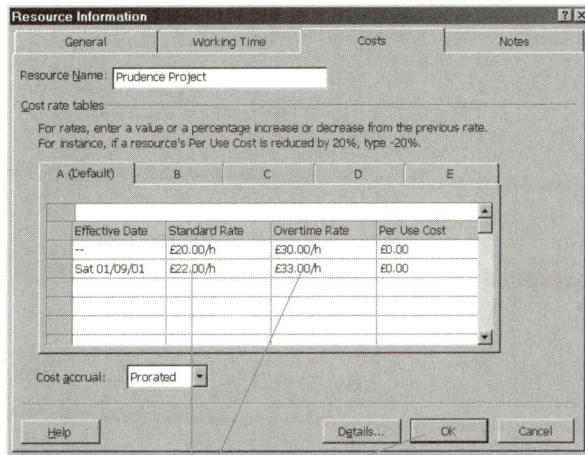

Note: you can also input a percentage figure for an increase (or a minus percentage for a decrease).

4 Type in the new standard and overtime rates and click OK.

Cost Rate Tables

In addition to being able to change cost rates, Project 2000 will also allow you to set up tables of rates for a resource. This can be useful if you need to use different rates for different types of work for the same person.

The cost rate tables are selected in the Costs tab in the Resource Information dialogue box:

1 In Resource Sheet view, double-click Bill Buggs. The Resource Information dialogue box opens.

2 Make sure the Costs tab is selected and click Tab B in the Cost rate tables area.

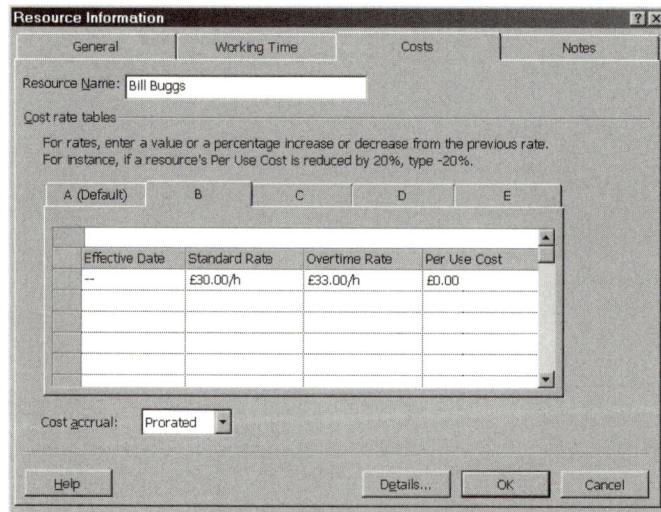

3 Type in the new standard rate '30' and new overtime rate '33'.

4 Click Tab A and verify that the default rates have not changed.

5 Click OK to save the new rates table.

Applying Resource Rates

Having set up the new Cost rate table in the previous topic, we can now apply it to any tasks where it is relevant:

1 Select View>Task Usage on the Menu Bar.

2 Select task 5 (Identify Business Case), select Bill Buggs and click the Go To Selected Task button (this moves the time scale to bring the selected task into view).

3 Click the Assignment Information button. The Assignment Information dialogue box opens. Select the General tab if required.

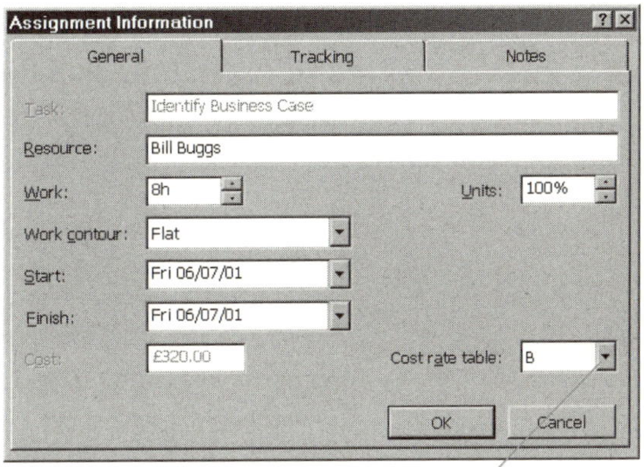

Assignment Information		? X
General	Tracking	Notes

Task: Identify Business Case

Resource: Bill Buggs

Work: 8h   Units: 100%

Work contour: Flat

Start: Fri 06/07/01

Finish: Fri 06/07/01

Cost: £320.00   Cost rate table: B

OK   Cancel

4 Click the Cost rate table down arrow and select Table B.

5 Click OK. The new cost rate table is assigned to the task for Bill Buggs and the costs for the task are recalculated on that basis.

The Business Case

Once you have identified all the costs for the project, it is a good idea to re-examine the business case. The business case is the reason or justification for carrying out the project in the first place and once all the costs are known (or at least estimated) it may be that there is no longer a clear business case. If this is the situation the project should be reconsidered.

The project manager should not be responsible for making or supporting the business case. This is the responsibility of the project sponsor. The project manager's role is to determine the real costs of the project so that the business can make the decision about the viability (or not) of the project.

The costs for a properly planned project will normally start fairly low and gradually build up through the life of the project. Planning should take place at the start of the project so that a reasonable idea of the likely cost is available before too much time and expenditure has taken place. Then if the decision is made to cancel the project the costs will still be fairly low.

So what should the business case consist of? Basically, just a statement of the expected costs and benefits, defined as:

- *Project Costs* – The costs of the project and any new systems implemented as a result of it over the number of years of expected life of the new systems. The new system could be a computer system or just a new way of working.

- *Project Benefits* – The benefits (expressed over the same time period) would represent any savings as a result of replacing an old system plus any other quantifiable business benefits (such as new business revenue).

While the project manager should be responsible for the project costs, the benefits and the decision to go ahead with the project should be defined by the business or the project sponsor on behalf of the business.

Project Calendars

This chapter explains what the various project calendars are, how to create them, set them up for the project and assign and change them for individual resources.

Covers

Chapter Eight

Calendars

Scheduling a project consists of allocating tasks to resources in line with their availability. So before you can start scheduling you need to know the availability and non-availability of the resources you will be using (e.g. if they are going to be on holiday or on a training course at any time during the project).

Project 2000 uses calendars to determine working and non-working days, default start time and the working hours in a day.

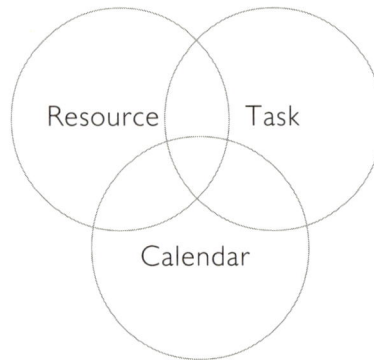

So resources, tasks and availability (the resource calendar) are all interlinked. If any change happens to one of them it can impact on the others and on the project schedule.

There are three types of calendar: base calendars, individual resource calendars and task calendars. Base calendars define the working days and hours for the whole project (or for a group of resources). Resource calendars define the working days and working hours for an individual resource. Task calendars define when a task can or cannot take place.

There are two other base calendars provided: the Night-Shift and 24-hour calendars.

The standard calendar is the default project base calendar. It defines the working days and hours for the whole project.

When a resource is added to a project, the standard calendar is allocated to that resource as its base calendar. Any changes made to the standard calendar are reflected in the resource calendars that are based on it.

...cont'd

The relationships between the various base calendars, the resource calendars and the project defaults require a little explanation.

If you consider them as three levels, they work like this:

1 Project Defaults are used by Project 2000 to set the duration and work of tasks, and in the allocation of resources.

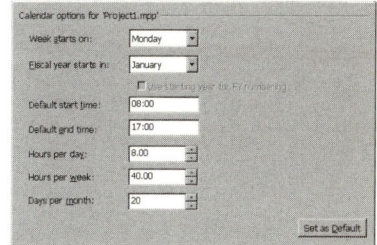

2 Base Calendars are used to define the working days and hours for the project (or a group of resources within the project).

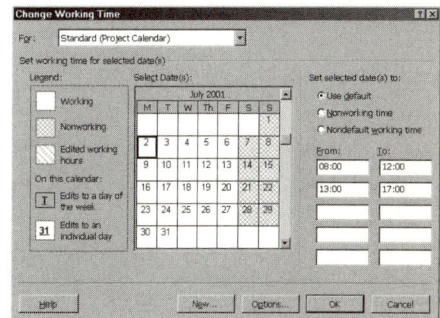

Project 2000 is supplied with the following three base calendars:

- *Standard*
- *Night Shift*
- *24-hour*

You can also create your own base calendars.

3 Resource Calendars are created for each resource and inherit their base calendar working days and hours. They are used to set any variations from the base calendar, such as annual holidays and meetings. Task calendars are similar.

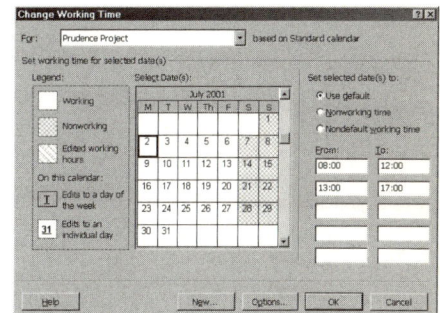

Project Defaults

Project defaults are initially set the same as the standard base calendar. Working time is Monday to Friday, 08:00 to 12:00 and 13:00 to 17:00 with no holidays.

Changing the project defaults does not change any of the base calendars or the resource calendars based on them.

Changing the project defaults will change the way that tasks are allocated duration and the way that resources are allocated to them.

If you make any changes to project defaults you must also change the relevant base calendar(s) to keep them in step:

Changes to the project defaults will not change base or resource calendars.

You can also click Tools> Options and select the Calendar tab.

If you are going to make any changes to the working hours you must do it before you start entering tasks. Once you have entered a task it will be based on the default hours at the time you entered it. If you want to try it out, save your project first, make the changes and see what happens to your schedule!

1 On the Menu Bar click Tools > Change Working Time. The Change Working Time dialogue box opens.

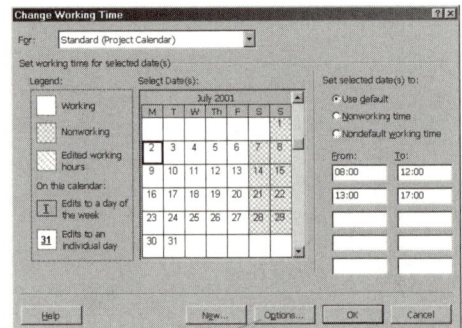

2 Click Options. The Options dialogue box opens at the Calendar tab.

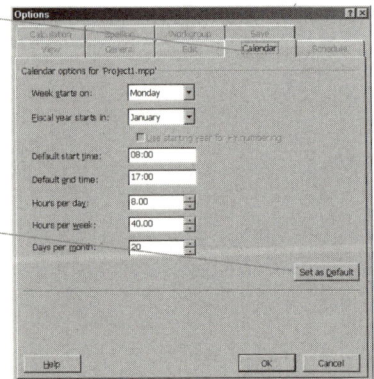

3 Make any required changes and click Set as Default.

4 If you have made any changes to the days or hours, make sure you make the same changes in your standard/base calendar and see the warning on the left.

Standard Calendar

Changing the default settings will not change any base calendar.

The standard calendar has a default setting of 08:00 (8 am) to 17:00 (5 pm) for the working hours and Monday to Friday (with no holidays) for the working days.

The first step is to set up the base calendar for your project by making any required changes to the working hours and working days and putting in public or other holidays.

The Change Working Time dialogue box is used to make these changes:

1 Click Tools>Change Working Time on the Menu Bar. The Change Working Time dialogue box appears:

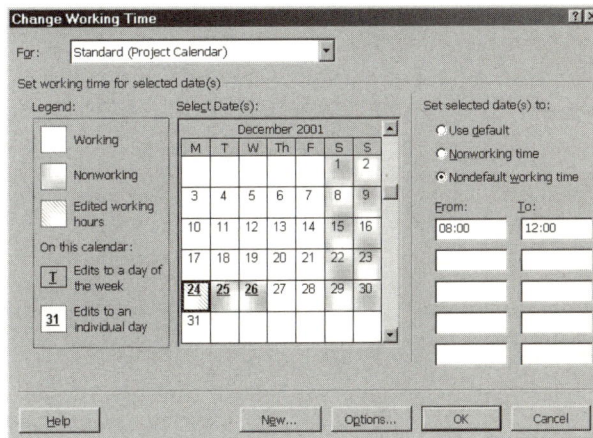

2 Change to August using the scrollbar, select Monday 27th and click 'Nonworking time'.

3 Change to December, select the 24th, click 'Non-default working time' and then delete the afternoon working time. You do this by selecting the second From time and deleting it and then the second To time.

4 Now change the 25th and 26th December and 1st January to 'Nonworking time' and click OK.

Creating a New Base Calendar

If none of the available base calendars fit the project requirements, or if you need a base calendar for a group of resources that work different hours, you can create a new one.

A new base calendar can be created from the project calendar defaults or by copying an existing base calendar. This will mean you don't have to redefine holidays, etc.

1 Open the Change Working Time dialogue box and click New. The Create New Base Calendar dialogue box opens:

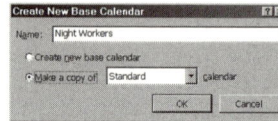

2 Type the name of the new base calendar as 'Night Workers', make sure 'Make a copy of Standard calendar' is selected and click OK. The new calendar is selected.

3 Select the day titles for T, W, Th and F by dragging across them. Then change the working hours to 00:00 to 05:00 and 21:00 to 00:00.

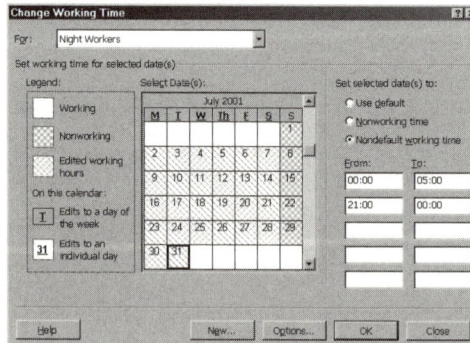

If you have people working shifts that span midnight (e.g., 21:00 to 05:00) the hours before midnight have to be entered on one day and the hours after midnight on the next.

4 Change Monday to 21:00 to 00:00 and Saturday to 00:00 to 05:00. Click OK.

Assigning a Calendar

If you create additional base calendars, they can then be assigned to the whole project or to individuals or groups of resources.

The base calendar can be assigned on the Resource Sheet or in the Resource Information dialogue box.

If you do not assign a base calendar, the standard calendar is assigned by default.

If changes have already been made to a resource calendar and a new base calendar is assigned to the resource, the changes will be retained and applied to the new base.

1   In Resource Sheet view double-click on Wendy Page.
     The Resource Information dialogue box opens.

2   Select the Working Time tab. (Note the Base Calendar is currently 'Standard'.)

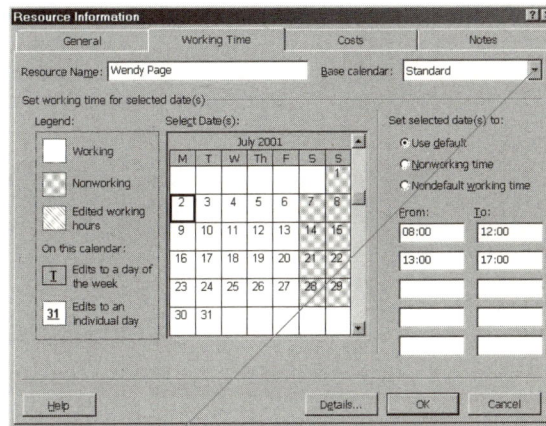

3   Click here, select 'Night Workers' and click OK.

Resource Name	Type	Material Label	Initials	Group	Max. Units	Std. Rate	Ovt. Rate	Cost/Use	Accrue At	Base Calendar
Prudence Project	Work		PP	Proj Mgr	100%	£20.00/hr	£30.00/hr	£0.00	Prorated	Standard
Joe Soap	Work		JS	Marketing	0%	£25.00/hr	£37.50/hr	£0.00	Prorated	Standard
Mary Dee	Work		MD	Accounts	100%	£15.00/hr	£22.50/hr	£0.00	Prorated	Standard
Wendy Page	Work		WP	IT	100%	£20.00/hr	£30.00/hr	£0.00	Prorated	Night Workers
Bill Buggs	Work		BB	Director	100%	£40.00/hr	£40.00/hr	£0.00	Prorated	Standard

Wendy Page is now working nights

Task Calendar

It will sometimes be necessary to define a task that can only take place at a certain time or on certain days. This is now possible in Project 2000 by using Task Calendars.

Let's say that you want to make a formal presentation to the company management who have a weekly management meeting on Friday mornings. You need to define the presentation as a task and then give it a task calendar with only Friday mornings as working time. We have a Report to Management (Task 20) in the project but this has a two day duration so we will need to split it into subtasks (activities).

1 Open your project in Gantt Chart view, insert two new tasks after Task 20 'Prepare Report' (1.5d) and 'Present to Management' (0.5d) and indent them.

	ⓘ	Task Name	Duration	Start	30 Jul 01	06 Aug 01
					M T W T F S S	M T W T
17		2.6 Evolve other recommendations	1 day	Tue 31/07/01		
18		2.7 Carry out risk analysis	2 days	Wed 01/08/01		
19		2.8 Produce forward plan	1 day	Fri 03/08/01		
20		⊟ **2.9 Report to management**	**2 days**	**Mon 06/08/01**		
21		2.9.1 Prepare report	1.5 days	Mon 06/08/01		
22		2.9.2 Present to management	0.5 days	Tue 07/08/01		
23		⊟ **3 Analysis Stage**	**15 days**	**Wed 08/08/01**		
24		3.1 Agree Requirements	5 days	Wed 08/08/01		

2 Now create a Management Meeting base calendar by selecting Tools>Change Working Time>New. The Create New Base Calendar dialogue box opens:

By making a copy of the standard base calendar it will inherit any public holidays and working time.

3 Select 'Make a Copy of Standard', call it 'Management Meetings' and click OK.

4 In the Change Working Time dialogue box select Monday to Thursday by dragging across the column headers and make them 'Nonworking time'.

5 Now select Friday, delete the afternoon time (it will change to 'Nondefault working time') and click OK.

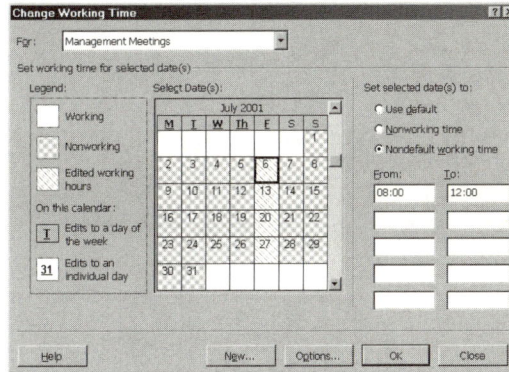

6 Double-click on Task 22 (Present to Management) to open the Task Information dialogue box, select the Advanced tab, select the Management Meetings calendar and click OK.

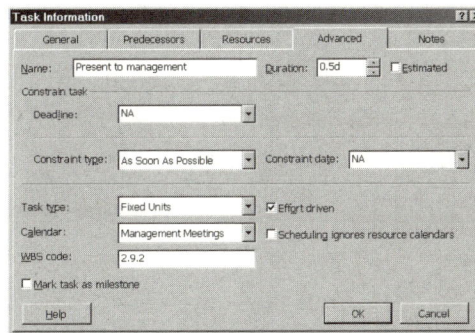

HOT TIP

To override the resource calendar for scheduling, select 'Scheduling ignores resource calendars'.

If a resource with a calendar is now assigned to the task, then the two calendars are combined for the purposes of scheduling when the task can take place.

Changing a Resource Calendar

Each resource is automatically assigned a calendar based on the standard calendar unless a different base calendar is specified. However, while that will include the standard working days and hours for the project it will not include times that the resource is unavailable at meetings, on holiday or attending a training course.

1 Open your project and select Resource Sheet view.

You can also double-click on a resource to open the associated Resource Information dialogue box.

2 Select 'Bill Buggs' and click the Resource Information button on the Toolbar.

3 Click the Working Time tab to display his resource calendar.

4 Use the scroll bar to move forward to August.

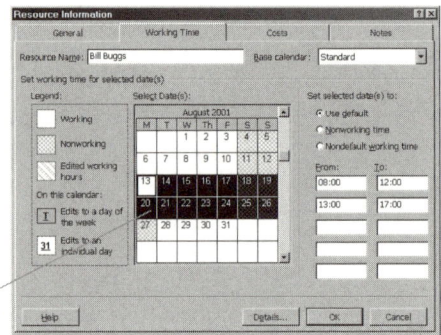

5 Drag to select the middle two weeks.

6 Change the setting in 'Set selected date(s) to:' to 'Nonworking time' and click on any day.

After step 6, the two weeks are shaded to indicate nonworking time and underlined to indicate they are an exception.

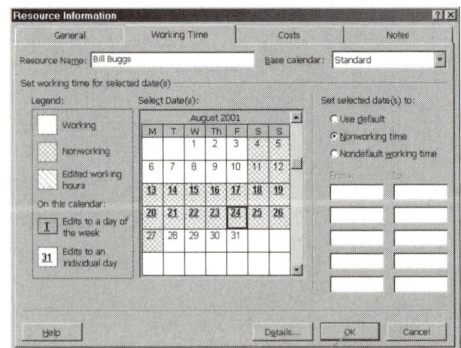

7 Click OK and save your project.

Project Scheduling

This chapter deals with scheduling a project and the effect of different task types on the scheduling process.

Covers

Chapter Nine

Scheduling

The process of scheduling uses the tasks, the resources allocated to them and their calendars to work out when tasks can be started, worked on and completed.

Forward Scheduling

The default approach to scheduling is to forward-schedule from a start date. You can also backward-schedule from a finish date.

The way that the schedule will be affected when resources, work effort or durations change is also dependent on the scheduling method and task types. The scheduling method can be either effort-driven or not. Tasks can be one of fixed-unit, fixed-duration or fixed-work.

Effort-driven Scheduling

This is the default scheduling method in Project 2000. In this method the duration of a task is adjusted to fit in with any changes to the resources. If a task is going to require 2 days' work effort and you allocate two resources to it (at 100%), it will be given a duration of 1 day.

If you then remove one of the resources, the additional day's work will be reallocated to the remaining resource and the duration will be extended to 2 days.

Note the following definitions which relate to scheduling:

- *Work is the effort that will be required to complete a task.*
- *Duration is the length of time that it will take to complete a task.*
- *Units are the resources that will be used to complete a task.*

You can turn effort-driven scheduling off for a specific task or for all new tasks. When effort-driven scheduling is turned off, adding an additional resource to a 2 day duration, fixed-unit task will increase the work by 2 days and the duration will remain unchanged.

Task Types

The task type (fixed-unit, fixed-duration or fixed-work) will determine what will be changed to accommodate any other changes. The basic equation used by Project 2000 is:

$$Work = Duration \times Units$$

where Units are resources and their percentage allocation.

Fixed-Unit Tasks

The fixed-unit task is the default task type in Project 2000. If resources are added or removed from a task, the duration is usually affected.

1 Click View>More Views from the Menu Bar, select Task Entry view and click Apply.

2 Select Task 14 (Feedback sessions) and click the Assign Resources button on the Toolbar.

3 Click your project manager and click Assign. Notice in the lower pane that 8 hours' work has been allocated to them.

4 Now assign Mary Dee to the task as well. (Notice that 4 hours' work is now allocated to each of them and the duration has halved.) Your screen should look something like the following:

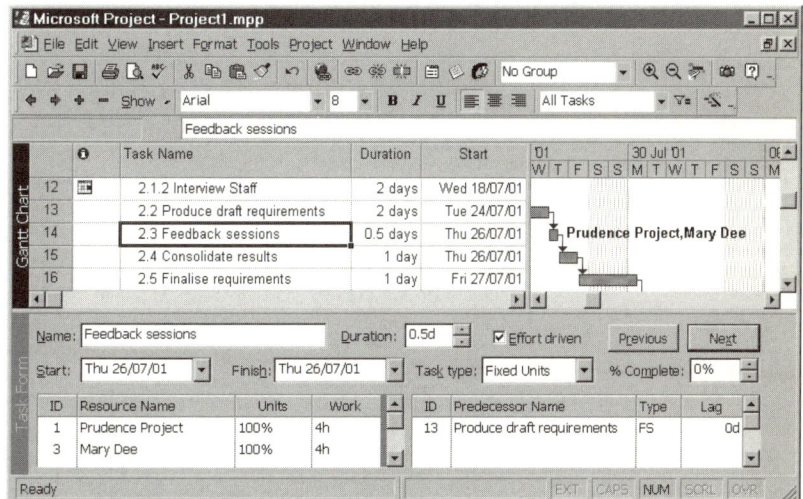

Most tasks will normally be fixed-unit tasks and you will want to be able to change the duration by assigning more resources to a task.

Fixed-Duration Tasks

If a task is a fixed-duration task, then (as the name implies) the duration remains fixed whether resources are added or removed. This has an impact on the way that scheduling takes place, depending on whether effort-driven scheduling is being used or not.

If effort-driven scheduling is being used this means that adding another resource to an existing task will split the work between the two resources. The effort will remain the same, the duration will remain the same so their units will be reduced to 50% to balance.

If effort-driven scheduling is not being used this means that adding another resource to an existing task will double the work. The duration stays the same, the units will be 100% so the work effort will double.

1   In Task Entry view, select Task 17 (Evolve Other Recommendations).

2   In the bottom pane change the task type to 'Fixed-Duration' and de-select 'Effort-Driven'.

3   In the top pane select Task 17 again and click the Allocate Resources button on the Toolbar.

4   Assign your project manager to the task (note at this time nothing has changed on the schedule).

5   Now assign Bill Buggs to the task. The bottom pane should look like the following:

Name: Evolve other recommendations		Duration: 1d	□ Effort driven	OK	Cancel
Start: Mon 30/07/01	Finish: Tue 31/07/01	Task type: Fixed Duration	% Complete: 0%		

ID	Resource Name	Units	Work	ID	Predecessor Name	Type	Lag
1	Prudence Project	100%	8h	16	Finalise requirements	FS	0d
5	Bill Buggs	100%	8h				

The duration has stayed the same (1 day), both people are allocated 100%, so the work effort has increased to 2 days.

Fixed-Work Tasks

The third task type is fixed-work. A fixed-work task must be effort-driven so only the duration and resource units can be affected.

Adding another resource will reduce the duration and increasing the duration will reduce the resource units.

1 In Task Entry view, in the top pane select Task 16 (Finalise Requirements).

2 In the bottom pane change the Task type to 'Fixed-Work' (notice 'Effort-Driven' de-selects) and click OK.

3 Re-select the task in the top pane and assign your project manager to it (note the work effort is 8 hours).

4 Now assign Bill Buggs to it (note that the work effort is still 8 hours so the duration halves to 0.5 days).

5 Now change the duration back to 1 day on the Task form (lower pane) and click OK. The resource units are both reduced to 50% so that the work effort remains at 8 hours. Your screen should look something like the following:

Contouring

When you assign a resource to a task, the total work is spread evenly throughout the duration of the task. This is referred to as a flat contour but there are a number of other contours that you can apply in Project 2000.

Contours can be applied or changed in Task Usage or Resource Usage views. In the former, the resources are grouped by task; in the latter, tasks are grouped by resource. In both cases the right-hand side of the screen displays the work values and is used to contour the work.

Contours are applied using the Assignment Information dialogue box. There are eight preset contours available:

Flat	Work hours are distributed evenly through the task duration.
Back Loaded	The hours start low and ramp up towards the end of the task.
Front Loaded	The hours start at 100% at the start of the task and tail off towards the end.
Double Peak	The hours peak twice during the task duration.
Early Peak	The hours peak during the first quarter of the task duration.
Late Peak	The hours peak during the last quarter of the task duration.
Bell	The hours start and finish low and peak in the middle of the task duration.
Turtle	Similar to Bell but the hours start and finish higher (i.e. there is less variation).

You can see the percentages that will be used by the different contours in Work Contour field (assignment field) from the Help Index.

Once a contour has been applied to a task, any changes to the task start or finish dates, the resources allocated or the duration will be applied using the contour.

HOT TIP *You can drag the heading dividers to increase or decrease the width of a field.*

1 Open your project in Resource Usage view and select Analyse the Risks (one of your project manager's tasks).

2 Click the Go To Selected Task button on the Toolbar to bring the task into view and adjust the screen to look like the example at the bottom of this page.

3 Click in the work field for the task and increase the 8 hours to 11 hours. The extra 3 hours are scheduled for the next working day.

4 Click the Assignment Information button on the Toolbar. The Assignment Information dialogue box opens:

Assignment Information	? X

General	Tracking	Notes

Task:	Analyse the Risks	
Resource:	Prudence Project	
Work:	11h	Units: 100%
Work contour:	Late Peak	
Start:	Mon 09/07/01	
Finish:	Tue 10/07/01	
Cost:	£220.00	Cost rate table: A

OK   Cancel

5 Click the Work contour down arrow, change the Work contour to Late Peak and click OK. The work contour changes and a contour indicator is added.

ⓘ	Resource Name	Work	Details	09 Jul 01 M	T	W	T	F
	⊟ Prudence Project	99 hrs	Work	1.8h	5.95h	5.25h	6h	
	Agree Project Objectives	8 hrs	Work					
	Identify Stakeholders	8 hrs	Work					
	Identify Project Team	8 hrs	Work					
	Identify Business Case	8 hrs	Work					
▁▂▃	Analyse the Risks	11 hrs	Work	1.8h	5.95h	3.25h		
	Produce Outline Project Plan	8 hrs	Work				2h	6h
▃▅▁	Interview Managers	16 hrs	Work					
	Feedback sessions	4 hrs	Work					

6 Save your project file and then try applying different contours to see the effect.

Resource Contouring

There is an inconsistency in the way this feature works, which is explained on the facing page.

Project 2000 includes a new feature that allows you to contour resource availability. This feature is aimed at situations where an individual is only available part time to a project with the percentage of their time available changing from period to period. Alternatively it would be applicable if a team of people were going to be working on a task or set of tasks and the team was going to have varying numbers of people available over time (perhaps building up the team initially and then releasing them in a phased way).

Applying a resource contour is quite straightforward:

1 Open your project in Resource Sheet view, select your project manager and open the Resource Information dialogue box at the General tab.

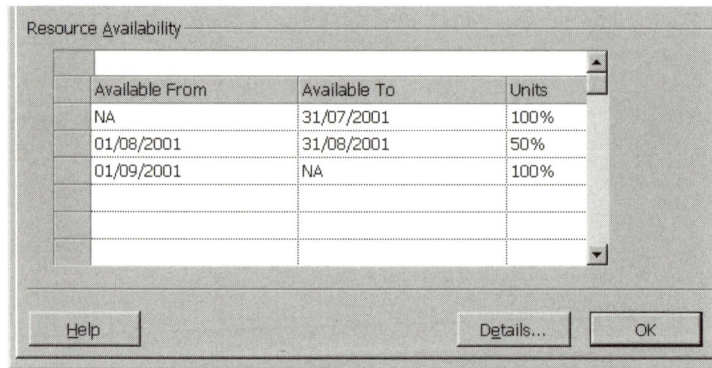

Resource Availability

Available From	Available To	Units
NA	31/07/2001	100%
01/08/2001	31/08/2001	50%
01/09/2001	NA	100%

Help   Details...   OK

2 Now enter the above availability profile for your project manager and click OK. Your project manager will be highlighted in red and a warning will be placed in the information column:

	ⓘ	Resource Name	Type	Material Label	Initials	Group	Max. Units
1	◈ ✛	Prudence Project	Work		PP	Proj Mgr	100%
2		◈ This resource should be leveled based on a Day by Day setting.			JS	Marketing	0%
3		Mary Dee	Work		MD	Accounts	100%

3   Now change to Gantt Chart view and select Task 18 (Carry out risk analysis) and click on the Go To Selected Task button to bring the Task bar into view.

4   Assign the task to your project manager and note what happens. It and the previous task have slipped right back into September and nothing is happening in August.

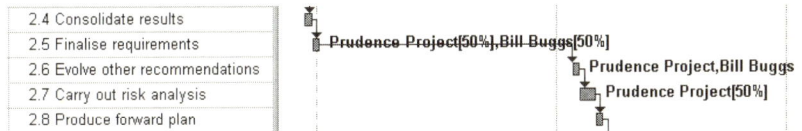

2.4 Consolidate results	
2.5 Finalise requirements	Prudence Project[50%],Bill Buggs[50%]
2.6 Evolve other recommendations	Prudence Project,Bill Buggs
2.7 Carry out risk analysis	Prudence Project[50%]
2.8 Produce forward plan	

This turns out to be caused by the fact that the project manager was originally assigned to Task 17 at 100%. When we entered the resource contour it did not change this task and it has now rescheduled it back to September when 100% of the resource is available again. The new assignment is correctly scheduled on 50% availability.

5   Select Task 17 (Evolve other recommendations) and click the Assign Resources button. Note the project manager is assigned 100%. Reduce this to 50%, press Enter and click Close. The problem has been resolved.

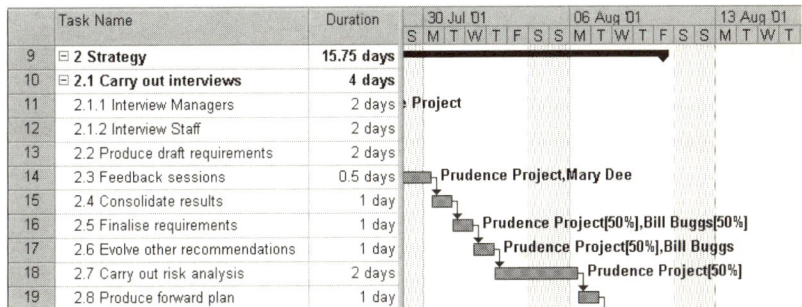

	Task Name	Duration	30 Jul 01	06 Aug 01	13 Aug 01
9	⊟ 2 Strategy	15.75 days			
10	⊟ 2.1 Carry out interviews	4 days			
11	2.1.1 Interview Managers	2 days	Project		
12	2.1.2 Interview Staff	2 days			
13	2.2 Produce draft requirements	2 days			
14	2.3 Feedback sessions	0.5 days	Prudence Project,Mary Dee		
15	2.4 Consolidate results	1 day			
16	2.5 Finalise requirements	1 day	Prudence Project[50%],Bill Buggs[50%]		
17	2.6 Evolve other recommendations	1 day	Prudence Project[50%],Bill Buggs		
18	2.7 Carry out risk analysis	2 days	Prudence Project[50%]		
19	2.8 Produce forward plan	1 day			

If you use resource contouring bear this issue in mind and check any tasks that are already assigned to the resource.

Backward Scheduling

The default method of scheduling is forward scheduling from the project start date. This is what we have been using so far. However, there are some times when you have to complete a project by a certain date in the future. By scheduling backwards from a finish date you can see when a project has to start. However, there is a right and a wrong way to go about it in Project 2000.

It is good practice to save your project before making any major changes to it. Just in case!

The Right Way

If you are going to use backward scheduling, then use it right from the start. When you first create your project set it to schedule from the required completion date:

Select Project>Project Information from the Menu bar, change Schedule from: to Project Finish Date, select your required finish date and click OK.

Then as you start to input your tasks and allocate resources Project 2000 will correctly backward-schedule your project. But what if you start off with forward scheduling and then decide you need to switch to backward scheduling?

The Wrong Way

Project 2000 will allow you to change from forward to backward scheduling but things are not always what they seem. If you want to try this save your project file first!

1 Open your project in Gantt Chart view, select Show Outline Level I (to hide all subtasks) and zoom out to get the whole project into view.

If you do have to change to backward scheduling, it is usually easier to start again with a new project file as per the Right Way above.

2 Select Project>Project Information from the Menu bar, change Schedule from: to Project Finish Date, select your required finish date and click OK.

3 Accept any warnings and carry on until the project is rescheduled. Sometimes it works and sometimes it doesn't.

Conflicts and Constraints

This chapter deals with resource conflicts, manual and automatic levelling and the use of task constraints. It also introduces setting a baseline and saving interim plans.

Covers

Chapter Ten

Resource Conflicts

As you begin to assign resources to tasks and then make subsequent changes to tasks and schedules, you will begin to get resource conflicts.

A resource conflict is where a resource is scheduled to perform more work than it can carry out in the time available. Project 2000 flags these conflicts for you by highlighting the relevant resource information in red and displaying a levelling indicator. Once these conflicts are identified the schedule needs to be examined and a decision made on how to resolve the conflict.

You can resolve these conflicts manually using Project 2000 scheduling or you can let Project 2000 automatically adjust the schedule by changing resources or task assignments for you. We will start by creating a resource conflict:

1 Open your project in Gantt Chart view and select Task 7 (Produce Outline Project Plan). Note the date it is currently scheduled for.

	❶	Task Name	Duration	Start	09 Jul 01 S M T W T F S	16 Jul 01 S M T W T F S
1		⊟ 1 Initiation	13.75 days	Mon 02/07/01		
2		1.1 Agree Project Objectives	1 day	Mon 02/07/01	ject	
3	◆	1.2 Identify Stakeholders	1 day	Tue 03/07/01	Project	
4		1.3 Identify Project Team	2 days	Wed 04/07/01	Buggs[50%],Prudence Project[50%]	
5		1.4 Identify Business Case	1 day	Fri 06/07/01	udence Project,Bill Buggs	
6		1.5 Analyse the Risks	2.75 days	Mon 09/07/01	Prudence Project	
7	📝	1.6 Produce Outline Project Plan	1 day	Wed 11/07/01	Prudence Project	
8		1.7 Project Approval	0 days	Thu 19/07/01		◆ 19/07

2 Open the Task Information dialogue box, select the Advanced tab, change the Constraint type to 'Finish No later Than', set the Constraint date to one day earlier than it currently is scheduled for and click OK.

3 In the Planning Wizard warning select the third option (Continue to set the constraint) and click OK. In the over allocation warning click Skip and in the second Planning Wizard warning select Continue and click OK.

We have now created a resource conflict for your project manager as Tasks 6 and 7 are both scheduled to happen at the same time.

5		1.4 Identify Business Case	1 day	Fri 06/07/01	Prudence Project,Bill Buggs
6		1.5 Analyse the Risks	2.75 days	Mon 09/07/01	Prudence Project
7		1.6 Produce Outline Project Plan	1 day	Tue 10/07/01	Prudence Project
8		1.7 Project Approval	0 days	Tue 17/07/01	17/07

4 Change to Resource Sheet view and notice that any over allocated resources are highlighted in red and have a warning symbol in the Information column.

	O	Resource Name	Type	Material Label	Initials	Group	Max. Units
1	◇	**Prudence Project**	**Work**		PP	**Proj Mgr**	**100%**
2		Joe Soap	Work		JS	Marketing	0%
3		Mary Dee	Work		MD	Accounts	100%
4		Wendy Page	Work		WP	IT	100%
5		Bill Buggs	Work		BB	Director	100%
6		Project Room	Material	Room		Facilities	
7		Personal Computer	Material	PC		Facilities	
8		Board Room	Material	Room		Facilities	
9		Overhead Projector	Material	OHP		Facilities	

5 From the Menu bar select View>Toolbars>Resource Management to open the Resource Management Toolbar.

6 Click the Resource Allocation view button on the Resource Management Toolbar.

7 Click the Go To Next Over Allocation button (third from the left).

The over allocation details are displayed in the view. The top pane shows the details of the problem: the project manager is going to have to work 13.95 hours in a single day. The lower pane shows a view of the Gantt Chart at the same level of detail. You can use the Go To Next Over Allocation button to view any more over allocations.

Resource Levelling

Resource conflicts can be resolved manually or automatically. The process used by Project 2000 to resolve conflicts is termed 'levelling'.

The Resource Leveling dialogue box is used to carry out levelling adjustments.

Always save your project before levelling. Then if anything goes wrong you can get back to where you were.

1 In Resource Allocation view, click Project>Project Information on the Menu bar. Note the current project finish date and click Cancel.

2 Select the lower (Leveling Gantt) pane so it is active.

3 Click Tools>Resource Leveling on the Menu bar. The Resource Leveling dialogue box opens:

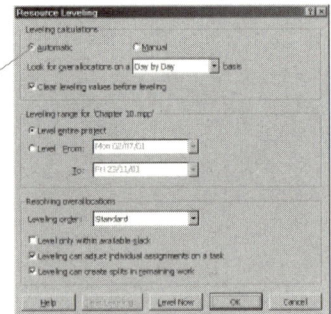

4 Select 'Automatic' and check the other options are as shown.

5 Click 'Level Now'. You will receive the following warning:

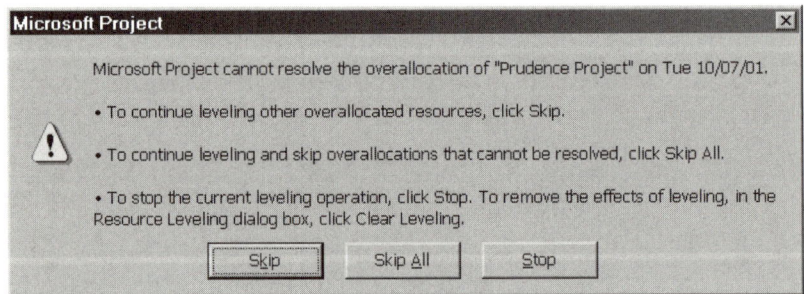

Microsoft Project

Microsoft Project cannot resolve the overallocation of "Prudence Project" on Tue 10/07/01.

• To continue leveling other overallocated resources, click Skip.

• To continue leveling and skip overallocations that cannot be resolved, click Skip All.

• To stop the current leveling operation, click Stop. To remove the effects of leveling, in the Resource Leveling dialog box, click Clear Leveling.

Skip   Skip All   Stop

6 Click Skip to continue levelling. When it is finished note the project finish date should not have changed. The project has been levelled without any slippage.

Manual Adjustments

In addition to using automatic resource levelling you also have to resolve some conflicts manually. You sometimes need to make manual adjustments to stop Project 2000 from automatically extending the schedule if it is unacceptable.

To manually resolve a conflict you will need to take steps such as the following:

• Allocating more resources to a task.

• Rescheduling or split a task.

• Adding overtime working.

• Reallocating tasks to a different resource.

1 In Gantt Chart view assign your project manager to all unallocated tasks (accept any warnings).

2 Click the Resource Allocation view button and then the Go To Next Over Allocation button on the Resource Management toolbar. Tasks 6 (Analyse the Risks) and 7 (Produce Outline Plan) are causing the over allocation.

The Assign Resources button is exactly the same as the one on the Standard Toolbar.

3 In the lower pane (Gantt Chart), select Task 6 (Analyse the Risks) and click the Assign Resources button on the Resource Management Toolbar.

4 Click Replace (to replace the current resource), select Mary Dee, click OK and click Close.

5 Select the upper pane (Resource Usage) and click the Go To Next Over Allocation button. By reallocating the task to a different resource you have removed the over allocation and resolved the conflict manually.

Task Constraints

When tasks are first entered into a project they have the project start date as their start date. As they are linked and have resources assigned to them, they will be scheduled depending on their dependencies and resource availability and be given their own start and finish dates.

Sometimes these allocated start and finish dates are not viable in the real world and a start or finish date has to be imposed. When this happens it is setting a 'task constraint'.

Task constraints are set in the form of start/finish on (or near) a particular date, no earlier/later than a particular date, or as soon/late as possible. The default constraint on a forward-scheduled project is 'As Soon As Possible' and this is applied to all tasks. For backward-scheduled projects the default constraint is 'As Late As Possible'.

Too many constraints will make it difficult to resolve schedule conflicts.

Constraints can be flexible or inflexible. A flexible constraint is one where the project finish date can be moved by the task. An inflexible constraint is one where the project finish date cannot be moved by the task. The following table lists the constraint types and whether they are flexible:

Constraint	Flexible for
'As Soon As Possible'	All projects
'As Late As Possible'	All projects
'Finish No Earlier Than'	Forward-scheduled projects
'Start No Earlier Than'	Forward-scheduled projects
'Finish No Later Than'	Backward-scheduled projects
'Start No Later Than'	Backward-scheduled projects

The first two constraints do not use a date, the others have a date associated with them. The date is the earliest or latest date that the task can start or finish (as appropriate to the constraint).

Applying Constraints

The usual reason for applying a constraint to a task is that some internal or external factor means it can only happen at a particular time.

For example if you did not want to start using a new accounting package until the start of the new year (1 January) you might well want to set a 'Start No Earlier Than' constraint:

1. In Gantt Chart view select Task 35 (Convert to New Package) and click the Go To Selected Task button.

2. Double-click the task and the Task Information dialogue box opens.

3. Select the General tab and note the current start and finish dates for the task.

4. Click the Advanced tab, select the 'Start No Earlier Than' constraint and select the date as 1 January 2002.

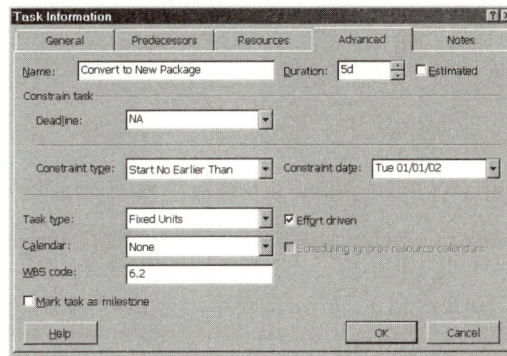

5. Click OK and accept any warnings. The constraint is set, the schedule adjusted and an indicator added.

Constraint Conflicts

If you set a constraint that causes a conflict, the Planning Wizard appears to warn you of the problem and offer suggestions where appropriate.

1 Save your project, then in Gantt Chart view double-click on Task 22 (Present to Management). The Task Information dialogue box opens.

2 Click the General tab and note the current finish date.

3 Click the Advanced tab and select 'Must Finish On' as the constraint.

4 Select the previous Friday's date (03/08/01) and click OK. The Planning Wizard dialogue box opens warning you of the scheduling conflict that could occur if you go ahead and set the constraint:

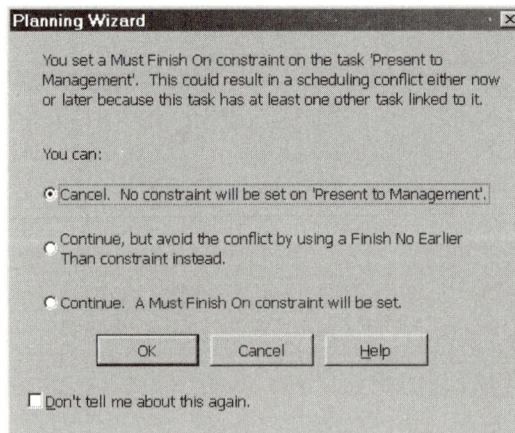

Planning Wizard

You set a Must Finish On constraint on the task 'Present to Management'. This could result in a scheduling conflict either now or later because this task has at least one other task linked to it.

You can:

○ Cancel. No constraint will be set on 'Present to Management'.

○ Continue, but avoid the conflict by using a Finish No Earlier Than constraint instead.

○ Continue. A Must Finish On constraint will be set.

[OK] [Cancel] [Help]

☐ Don't tell me about this again.

Do not do this unless you have saved your project first.

5 Normally you should cancel. As long as you have saved your project file, select Continue and click OK.
You will get a further scheduling conflict warning. If you still continue the schedule will be updated but Task 22 needs to start before Task 21 is completed!

Viewing Constraints

When a task has a constraint applied in Project 2000 there will be an indicator present. If you pause your cursor over it a pop-up will display details of the constraint. In addition, a flexible constraint will have a blue dot and an inflexible constraint a red dot.

You can also see constraints via the Constraints Date Table:

1. Open your project in Gantt Chart view and pause your cursor over the indicator on Task 7 (Produce Outline Project Plan), an inflexible constraint (see the red dot). The constraint details appear in a pop-up box (plus any notes).

2. Do the same for Task 35 (Convert to New Package) which has a blue dot.

3. Select View > More Views > Task Sheet from the Menu bar and then click Apply.

4. Select View > Table > More Tables from the Menu bar. The More Tables dialogue box appears.

5. Select Constraint Dates and click Apply. The Constraint Dates Table is displayed:

	Task Name	Duration	Constraint Type	Constraint Date
1	⊟ Initiation	12 days	As Soon As Possible	NA
2	Agree Project Objectives	1 day	As Soon As Possible	NA
3	Identify Stakeholders	1 day	As Soon As Possible	NA
4	Identify Project Team	2 days	As Soon As Possible	NA
5	Identify Business Case	1 day	As Soon As Possible	NA
6	Analyse the Risks	2.75 days	As Soon As Possible	NA
7	Produce Outline Project Plan	1 day	Finish No Later Than	Tue 10/07/01
8	Project Approval	0 days	As Soon As Possible	NA
9	⊞ Strategy	17.5 days	As Soon As Possible	NA
23	⊞ Analysis	20.5 days	As Soon As Possible	NA
28	⊞ Design	10 days	As Soon As Possible	NA
30	⊞ Build	30 days	As Soon As Possible	NA
33	⊟ Implement	56 days	As Soon As Possible	NA
34	Train Users	5 days	As Soon As Possible	NA
35	Convert to New Package	5 days	Start No Earlier Than	Tue 01/01/02
36	Change Budget	10 days	As Soon As Possible	NA

Setting a Baseline

Once you have created your project plan, allocated resources, resolved any conflicts and are happy with the project schedule, you are ready to set a baseline.

The baseline represents a record of a set point in time where you have agreed and fixed your project plan.

That is not to say that things won't change during the project – they undoubtedly will – but you will then be able to compare how things actually worked out with how they were planned.

When you set a baseline the dates, times and other data are recorded for all tasks.

1   Open your project in Gantt Chart view.

2   Select Tools > Tracking > Save Baseline from the Menu bar. The Save Baseline dialogue box opens:

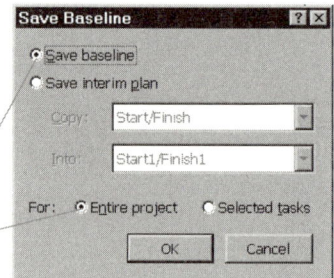

3   Select the 'Save baseline' and 'Entire project' options.

4   Click OK. The project is now baselined.

5   Select Project > Project Information from the Menu bar and click Statistics on the dialogue box. This shows the project's current, baseline and actual details.

Interim Plans

As well as setting a baseline (which should be retained throughout the project) you can also create up to ten interim plans during the project.

You may wish to create new interim plans at the end of each project stage to reflect any changes to the project that have been agreed. Or you may wish to produce interim plans to reflect possible changes to the project.

For longer projects it will be particularly useful as things do change with time and the use of interim plans will enable you to backtrack to where the project changed direction.

Interim plans hold start and finish dates for each task.

1   Select Tools > Tracking > Save Baseline from the Menu bar. The Save Baseline dialogue box appears.

2   Select 'Save Interim plan'; 'Copy: Start/Finish'; 'Into: Start1/Finish1'; and 'Entire project'. Click OK.

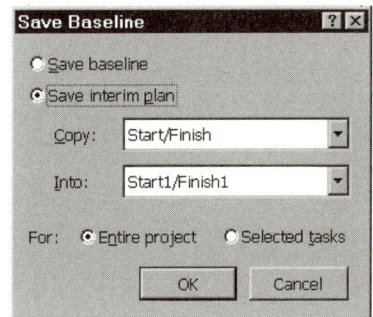

3   As your project progresses you can copy into Start2/Finish2 and so on.

4   You can also update interim plans by copying over a previous interim plan in 'Copy Into'.

At the end of the project you will be able to look back at the interim plans as well as the original baseline as part of your post-implementation review.

Clearing a Baseline

In previous versions of Microsoft Project there was no easy method for clearing the baseline data for a project. This was particularly true for time-based data. With Project 2000 you can now clear the baseline or interim plan data for the whole project or selected tasks.

1 From the Menu bar select Tools>Tracking>Clear Baseline. The Clear Baseline dialogue box opens:

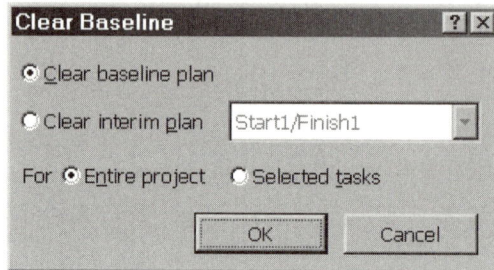

Clear Baseline	? X
⦿ Clear baseline plan	
○ Clear interim plan	Start1/Finish1 ▾
For ⦿ Entire project ○ Selected tasks	
OK	Cancel

2 Select 'Clear baseline plan', select 'Entire project' and click OK. The baseline is removed (select Project>Project Information and click Statistics to confirm).

3 In Gantt Chart view select Tasks 33 to 36 (the Implementation Stage) and reopen the Clear Baseline dialogue box (as above).

4 Select 'Clear interim plan', 'Start 1/Finish 1' and 'Selected tasks' and click OK. The interim plan is removed for the selected tasks. We will see more of this in a later topic.

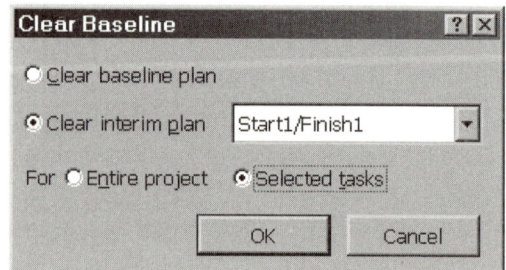

Clear Baseline	? X
○ Clear baseline plan	
⦿ Clear interim plan	Start1/Finish1 ▾
For ○ Entire project ⦿ Selected tasks	
OK	Cancel

Viewing Data

Project 2000 holds a vast amount of data or information on your project but you cannot see it all at the same time. It provides many options for selecting and viewing just the data you want at any particular time. This chapter covers the different ways of viewing, grouping, filtering and sorting data and how to tailor views to your specific project requirements.

Covers

Chapter Eleven

Views

In Project 2000, views can be placed into two main categories: task views and resource views. There are 20 task views and six resource views. You normally use task views when working with task information and resource views when working with resource information. The views can be further divided into sheets, charts, graphs and forms.

Sheets

Sheets display information in rows and columns (similar to a spreadsheet program) with each task or resource being a row (horizontal) and each field in the task or resource being a column (vertical).

Charts and Graphs

Charts display graphical information in chart form, typical examples being the Gantt Chart and Network Diagram views. Graphs are used to display statistical information graphically.

Forms

Forms are used for the display and entry of detailed information on a task or resource.

Some views (such as Calendar) are simple single views and some are compound views (such as Gantt Chart which shows a sheet on the left and a chart on the right). You can also display a single view in the Project 2000 window or two views (one above the other) as a combination view (such as Task Entry which shows the Gantt Chart above and Task Form below).

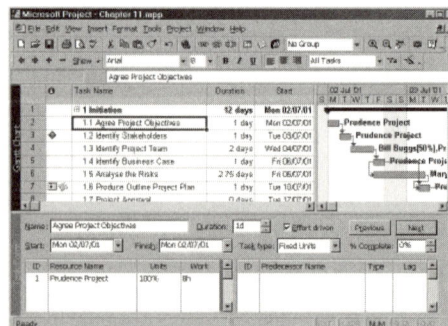

Tables

When working in Project 2000 in a sheet view there are a number of preset tables that can be used (applied) to access different types of information on tasks or resources. There are 19 task tables that can be applied to task views and 10 resource tables that can be applied to resource views.

If the view you have currently selected is not displaying quite the right information you can apply a different table to change the view. The tasks or resources displayed remain the same but you will see different bits of information for them.

Open your project in Gantt Chart view and select View>Table:Cost from the Toolbar. The Cost Table displays:

	Task Name	Fixed Cost	Fixed Cost Accrual	Total Cost	02 Jul 01	09 Jul 01
					S M T W T F S S	M T W T F S
1	⊟ 1 Initiation	£0.00	Prorated	£1,525.00		
2	1.1 Agree Project Objectiv	£0.00	Prorated	£160.00	Prudence Project	
3	1.2 Identify Stakeholders	£0.00	Prorated	£160.00	Prudence Project	
4	1.3 Identify Project Team	£0.00	Prorated	£480.00	Bill Buggs[50%],Prudence
5	1.4 Identify Business Case	£0.00	Prorated	£400.00	Prudence Project,Bill E
6	1.5 Analyse the Risks	£0.00	Prorated	£165.00	Mary Dee
7	1.6 Produce Outline Proje	£0.00	Prorated	£160.00	Prudence I
8	1.7 Project Approval	£0.00	Prorated	£0.00		

2 Switch to Task Usage view and select View>Table: Work from the Toolbar. The Work Table displays:

	Task Name	Work	Baseline	Variance	Actual	Details	02 Jul 02 M	T	W
1	⊟ Initiation	67 hrs	0 hrs	67 hrs	0 hrs	Work	8h	8h	8h
2	⊟ Agree Project Objectives	8 hrs	0 hrs	8 hrs	0 hrs	Work	8h		
	Prudence Project	8 hrs	0 hrs	8 hrs	0 hrs	Work	8h		
3	⊟ Identify Stakeholders	8 hrs	0 hrs	8 hrs	0 hrs	Work		8h	
	Prudence Project	8 hrs	0 hrs	8 hrs	0 hrs	Work		8h	
4	⊟ Identify Project Team	16 hrs	0 hrs	16 hrs	0 hrs	Work			8h
	Prudence Project	8 hrs	0 hrs	8 hrs	0 hrs	Work			4h
	Bill Buggs	8 hrs	0 hrs	8 hrs	0 hrs	Work			4h
5	⊟ Identify Business Case	16 hrs	0 hrs	16 hrs	0 hrs	Work			
	Prudence Project	8 hrs	0 hrs	8 hrs	0 hrs	Work			
	Bill Buggs	8 hrs	0 hrs	8 hrs	0 hrs	Work			

3 Try applying the various different tables to the views that you use to see what is available. When you have finished apply the default (Entry) tables again.

Grouping

Grouping allows you to view your project tasks or resources grouped by any defined criteria. This can be applied to most task and resource views but not Calendar, Network Diagram, Relationship Diagram, Resource Graph and Form views. Each view has various standard groups to select from.

1. Open your project in Resource Sheet view and click the down arrow to the right of the Group By field.

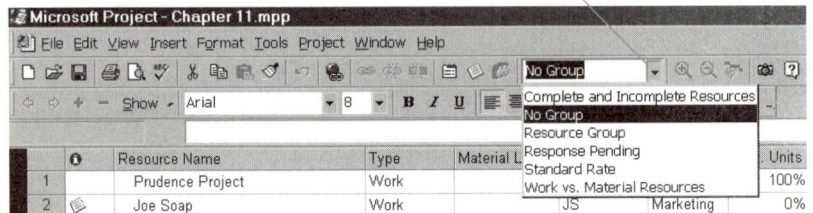

2. Select Resource Group and the Resource Sheet is rearranged by Resource within Group:

3. Try selecting the other 'Group By' options from the drop down list and finally re-select No Groups to return to the standard Resource Sheet view.

4. Now change to Gantt Chart view, select Show>Outline Level 1, then select Group By>Constraint Type. Note that all non-summary tasks are now displayed but no summary tasks; in their place the Constraint types are displayed.

	ⓘ	Task Name	Duration	Start	Jul 01 02 09 16 23 30	Aug 01 06 13 20 27
		⊞ Constraint Type: As Soon As Possible	146 days	Mon 02/07/01	▼	
		⊟ Constraint Type: Finish No Later Than	1 day	Tue 10/07/01	▼	
7	⊡◇	1.6 Produce Outline Project Plan	1 day	Tue 10/07/01	▯ Prudence Project	
		⊟ Constraint Type: Start No Earlier Than	123 days	Thu 19/07/01	▼	
12	⊡	2.1.2 Interview Staff	2 days	Thu 19/07/01	▯ Prudence Project	
35	⊡	6.2 Convert to New Package	5 days	Tue 01/01/02		

This is a useful view to see which constraints you have set on which tasks. The group 'summary tasks' behave in the same way as the normal summary tasks and the view can be expanded and contracted by clicking the small plus or minus sign beside the group name.

The other useful feature is that Project 2000 rolls up totals by these groupings for you which is useful for monitoring costs and work effort.

5 Select Gantt Chart view and then select Group By>Critical. The new grouping is applied to the Gantt Chart.

6 Now select View>Table:Work from the Menu bar. The rolled up work effort totals are displayed on the Critical and non-critical summary lines.

	Task Name	Work	Baseline	Variance	Actual	Jul 01 25 02 09 16 23 30	Aug 01 06 13 20 27	Sep 0 03 10
	⊟ Critical: Yes	187 hrs	0 hrs	187 hrs	0 hrs	▼		
2	1.1 Agree Project Objectives	8 hrs	0 hrs	8 hrs	0 hrs	▯ Prudence Project		
3	1.2 Identify Stakeholders	8 hrs	0 hrs	8 hrs	0 hrs	▯ Prudence Project		
4	1.3 Identify Project Team	16 hrs	0 hrs	16 hrs	0 hrs	▯ Bill Buggs[50%],Prudence Proje		
5	1.4 Identify Business Case	16 hrs	0 hrs	16 hrs	0 hrs	▯ Prudence Project,Bill Buggs		
6	1.5 Analyse the Risks	11 hrs	0 hrs	11 hrs	0 hrs	▯ Mary Dee		
7	1.6 Produce Outline Project Plan	8 hrs	0 hrs	8 hrs	0 hrs	▯ Prudence Project		
35	6.2 Convert to New Package	40 hrs	0 hrs	40 hrs	0 hrs			
36	6.3 Change Budget	80 hrs	0 hrs	80 hrs	0 hrs			

HOT TIP

You probably won't want to use most of the Group By options but it is worth knowing what is available.

7 Now try out the other Group By options on the Gantt Chart view and finally try the options on other views.

Customised Groups

While there are a good number of standard 'Group By' options built into the standard views you may also wish to define your own custom groups. You can define these based on a single or multiple criteria. Finally the colour, pattern and font of the group bands can be customised along with the sequence of sorting:

1   Open your project in Gantt Chart view and select Project>Group By>Customise Group By from the Menu bar. The Customise Group By dialogue box opens.

2   Select the first Field Name field and select Resource Names from the list. Select the second Field Name and select Critical from the list. Click OK to create the custom group.

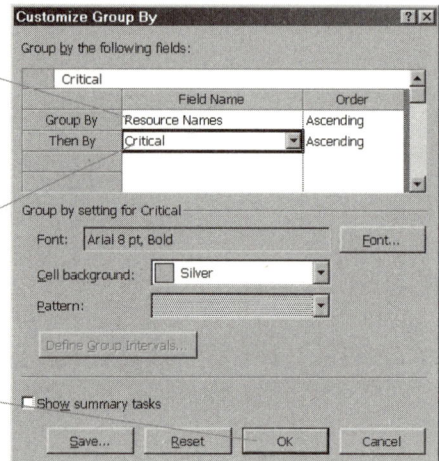

3   The dialogue box can also be used to define the font, background and pattern of the group summary tasks. Numerical fields can also be grouped by using the Define Group Intervals button.

Fiscal Year

Project 2000 now allows you to set the use of the fiscal year for both the major (upper) and minor (lower) timescales. This feature is useful where the business (fiscal) year is different from the calendar year.

1   Open your project in Gantt Chart view and select Tools>Change Working Time>Options from the Menu bar. The Options dialogue box opens:

2   Change 'Fiscal year starts in' to April, select 'Use starting year for FY numbering' and click OK. Click OK again to close the Options dialogue box.

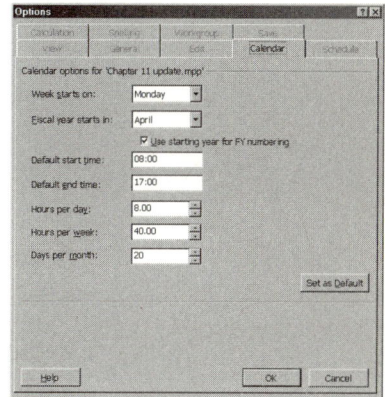

You can also get the Timescale dialogue box by double-clicking on the timescale on the Gantt Chart.

3   Select Format> Timescale from the Menu bar. The Timescale dialogue box opens:

4   Set the major scale to Years and de-select Use Fiscal Year. Set the minor scale to Quarters and select Use Fiscal Year.

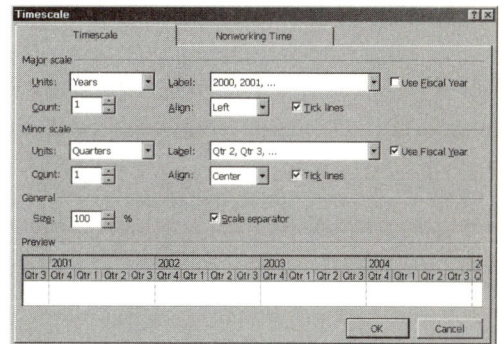

Click OK. The major timescale now displays calendar years and the minor scale displays fiscal Quarters (as shown in Preview).

Filters

In addition to its other selection capabilities, Project 2000 also allows you to filter and sort data before viewing (or printing). Filtering allows you to select just the information that you wish to be displayed.

There are a number of pre-defined filters that you can use to select things such as late tasks, tasks in progress, work that is over budget, and so on. Project 2000 actually contains 32 pre-defined task filters and 23 pre-defined resource filters. In addition you can also create your own custom filters to meet the specific requirements of your project.

Filters can be used to focus on specific tasks in your project or on specific resources in the project. When you apply a filter only the tasks or resources that meet the filter criteria are displayed. All other tasks and resources are hidden while you are using a filter.

Applying filters to your project does not change the data in any way, it just changes the way you are viewing it.

Project 2000 contains an AutoFilter feature which gives you a quick way of finding particular information in a field. When it's turned on, each column heading has an arrow on the right hand side which can be used to apply a filter to the information in the column. You can apply filters to as many columns as you like and once a filter is applied to a column, the column title turns blue.

As well as specific filters you can apply interactive filters which display a dialogue box during the filtering process. You then provide the information to the dialogue box to allow it to complete the filtering process.

If none of the pre-defined filters meet your requirements you can create a custom filter that exactly matches your needs. You can copy an existing filter and then edit it to meet your needs or you can create a completely new filter. The Filter Definition dialogue box provides shortcuts to simplify this process.

AutoFilter

When AutoFilter is turned on you can apply filters to any column. Use the 'All...' filter to remove any filter criteria and use the Custom filter to filter a column by more than one criterion.

1 Open your project in Task Sheet view and view all subtasks.

2 Select View > Table > Usage from the Menu bar. The relevant columns are displayed.

You can save an AutoFilter as a Custom filter for future reuse.

3 Click the AutoFilter button on the Toolbar. Down arrows appear on column headings:

	ⓘ	Task Name ▾	Work ▾	Duration ▾	Start ▾	Finish ▾
1		⊟ **Initiation**	**67 hrs**	**12 days**	**Mon 02/07/01**	**Tue 17/07/01**
2		Agree Project Objectives	8 hrs	1 day	Mon 02/07/01	Mon 02/07/01
3	◆	Identify Stakeholders	8 hrs	1 day	Tue 03/07/01	Tue 03/07/01
4		Identify Project Team	16 hrs	2 days	Wed 04/07/01	Thu 05/07/01
5		Identify Business Case	16 hrs	1 day	Fri 06/07/01	Fri 06/07/01
6		Analyse the Risks	11 hrs	2.75 days	Fri 06/07/01	Tue 10/07/01
7	⊡✎	Produce Outline Project Plan	8 hrs	1 day	Tue 10/07/01	Tue 10/07/01
8		Project Approval	0 hrs	0 days	Tue 17/07/01	Tue 17/07/01

4 Click the Duration down arrow and select '> I day' (greater than I day). The view changes to only display tasks greater than I day's duration and the column heading is displayed in blue. Change it back to (All).

5 Click the Work down arrow and select 'Custom'. The Custom Auto Filter dialogue box opens. In Work, select 'is greater than...'. Select 12h. Click OK. The display is filtered accordingly.

6 Click the AutoFilter button on the Toolbar again to turn it off. All tasks are displayed again.

Filter Criteria

You can specify filter criteria interactively if you often want to make a similar enquiry but with slightly different parameters. This is preferable to creating a large number of custom filters.

For example, you might want to get details of all tasks during the summer to check for any holiday implications:

1 Open your project in Task Sheet view and select View>Table>Schedule from the Menu bar.

2 Select Project>Filtered for>Date Range from the Menu bar. The Date Range dialogue box opens:

3 Type 01/08/01 and click OK. The Date Range dialogue box opens again for the end date.

Date Range

Show tasks that start or finish after:

OK   Cancel

4 Type 31/08/01 and click OK. Only tasks that are due to be in progress during August are listed:

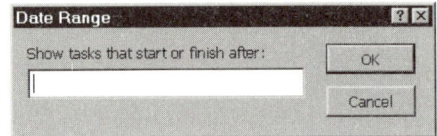

	Task Name	Start	Finish	Late Start	Late Finish
9	⊟ **Strategy**	**Wed 18/07/01**	**Fri 10/08/01**	**Mon 10/09/01**	**Fri 28/09/01**
18	Carry out risk analysis	Tue 31/07/01	Thu 02/08/01	Fri 21/09/01	Tue 25/09/01
19	Produce forward plan	Thu 02/08/01	Fri 03/08/01	Tue 25/09/01	Wed 26/09/01
20	⊟ **Report to management**	**Fri 03/08/01**	**Fri 10/08/01**	**Wed 26/09/01**	**Fri 28/09/01**
21	Prepare Report	Fri 03/08/01	Mon 06/08/01	Wed 26/09/01	Thu 27/09/01
22	Present to Management	Fri 10/08/01	Fri 10/08/01	Fri 28/09/01	Fri 28/09/01
23	⊟ **Analysis**	**Fri 10/08/01**	**Fri 07/09/01**	**Mon 01/10/01**	**Mon 29/10/01**
24	Agree Requirements	Fri 10/08/01	Fri 17/08/01	Mon 01/10/01	Fri 05/10/01
25	Select Package	Fri 17/08/01	Fri 24/08/01	Mon 08/10/01	Fri 12/10/01

5 Click the Filter down arrow on the Toolbar and select All Tasks. All tasks are again displayed.

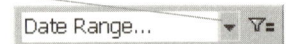

Date Range...

Filter by Resource

You can use resource filters to display tasks assigned to a resource. You can also use resource filters to change the resource information for one or more resources.

If the Facilities Group was going to change its name to Premises and you wanted to change all resources, you could use the resource filter to filter by that group name and then change it for all resources in the group.

1   Open your project in Resource Sheet view.

2   Click the Filter down arrow on the Toolbar and select Group... (the ellipsis indicates further choices). The Group dialogue box opens.

3   Type in 'Facilities' and click OK. Now only the four Facilities resources are displayed.

4   Click the Resource Name column heading to select all resources. Then click the Resource Information button on the Toolbar. The Multiple Resource Information dialogue box opens.

5   On the General tab, click in the Group field, type 'Premises' and click OK. Accept any warnings. All resources will have their Group changed to Premises.

	Resource Name	Type	Material Label	Initials	Group	Max. Units	Std. Rate	Ovt. Rate
6	Project Room	Material	Room		Premises		£0.00	
7	Personal Computer	Material	PC		Premises		£0.00	
8	Board Room	Material	Room		Premises		£0.00	
9	Overhead Projector	Material	OHP		Premises		£0.00	

Custom Filters

Custom filters can be created from new or they can be created from an existing filter. The easiest way is to make a copy of an existing filter and then edit it.

The Filter Definition dialogue box is used to name the filter, select the settings and define the criteria. A filter can have a single criterion or multiple criteria. Where multiple criteria are used they have to be separated by operators such as 'And' and 'Or' ('And' means both criteria must be met, 'Or' means either or both can be met).

1   Open your project in Gantt Chart view and select Project> Filtered For>More Filters. The More Filters dialogue box opens (this lists all filters).

HOT TIP

To copy an existing filter click Copy in the More Filters dialogue box.

2   Click New. The Filter Definition dialogue box opens.

3   Type the name 'Start after 1 Sept' and select 'Show in menu'.

4   Click in the first row under Field Name, click the down arrow and select 'Start'.

5   Click in the Test column, click the down arrow and select 'is greater than or equal to'.

6   Click in the Value(s) column and type '01/09/01' and click OK. The new filter is shown in the More Filters dialogue box.

HOT TIP

The new filter is also now shown in the drop down range list on the Toolbar.

7   Click Apply and only the tasks from September are displayed.

Sorting

Tasks and resources are usually displayed in ascending ID Number order. However, you can sort by any field or even a combination of fields by specifying sort keys.

1 Open your project in Task Sheet view and show all subtasks.

2 Select View > Table > Usage from the Menu bar.

3 Select Project > Sort > Sort By from the Menu bar. The Sort dialogue box opens.

4 Click the 'Sort by' down arrow, select 'Summary' and select 'Descending'. Click the 'Then by' down arrow, select 'Duration' and select 'Descending'. De-select 'Keep outline structure' and click Sort. The summary tasks are sorted first in descending sequence followed by the subtasks in descending sequence.

Combining sorting with filters gives you a powerful range of options.

	❶	Task Name	Work	Duration	Start	Finish
33		⊟ Implement	160 hrs	56 days	Mon 05/11/01	Mon 21/01/02
30		⊟ Build	240 hrs	30 days	Mon 24/09/01	Fri 02/11/01
23		⊟ Analysis	80 hrs	20.5 days	Fri 10/08/01	Fri 07/09/01
9		⊟ Strategy	104 hrs	17.5 days	Wed 18/07/01	Fri 10/08/01
1		⊟ Initiation	67 hrs	12 days	Mon 02/07/01	Tue 17/07/01
28		⊟ Design	80 hrs	10 days	Mon 10/09/01	Fri 21/09/01
20		⊟ Report to management	8 hrs	5 days	Fri 03/08/01	Fri 10/08/01
10		⊟ Carry out interviews	32 hrs	4 days	Wed 18/07/01	Mon 23/07/01
32		Change Budget	200 hrs	25 days	Mon 01/10/01	Fri 02/11/01
29		Change Budget	80 hrs	10 days	Mon 10/09/01	Fri 21/09/01
36		Change Budget	80 hrs	10 days	Tue 08/01/02	Mon 21/01/02
24		Agree Requirements	20 hrs	5 days	Fri 10/08/01	Fri 17/08/01
25		Select Package	20 hrs	5 days	Fri 17/08/01	Fri 24/08/01
31		Install Package	40 hrs	5 days	Mon 24/09/01	Fri 28/09/01
34		Train Users	40 hrs	5 days	Mon 05/11/01	Fri 09/11/01
35	▥	Convert to New Package	40 hrs	5 days	Tue 01/01/02	Mon 07/01/02

Highlight Filters

When tasks and resources are filtered those that do not meet the criteria are hidden from view. Highlight filters can be used so that all tasks or resources are still visible but the tasks or resources that meet the criteria are highlighted in blue.

1 Open your project in Gantt Chart view and show all subtasks.

2 Select Project>Filter For>More Filters.

3 In the More Filters dialogue box select 'Resource Group...' and click Highlight.

4 The tasks with a resource in the 'Director' group (tasks 4, 5, 16 and 17) are highlighted in blue.

	0	Task Name	Duration	Start	Jul 01 / Aug 01 / Sep 01 / Oct 01
1		⊟ 1 Initiation	12 days	Mon 02/07/01	
2		1.1 Agree Project Objectives	1 day	Mon 02/07/01	Prudence Project
3	◆	1.2 Identify Stakeholders	1 day	Tue 03/07/01	Prudence Project
4		1.3 Identify Project Team	2 days	Wed 04/07/01	Bill Buggs[50%],Prudence Project[50%]
5		1.4 Identify Business Case	1 day	Fri 06/07/01	Prudence Project,Bill Buggs
6		1.5 Analyse the Risks	2.75 days	Fri 06/07/01	Mary Dee
7	⊞🖉	1.6 Produce Outline Project Plan	1 day	Tue 10/07/01	Prudence Project
8		1.7 Project Approval	0 days	Tue 17/07/01	◆ 17/07
9		⊟ 2 Strategy	17.5 days	Wed 18/07/01	
10		⊟ 2.1 Carry out interviews	4 days	Wed 18/07/01	
11		2.1.1 Interview Managers	2 days	Wed 18/07/01	Prudence Project
12	📷	2.1.2 Interview Staff	2 days	Thu 19/07/01	Prudence Project
13		2.2 Produce draft requirements	2 days	Tue 24/07/01	Prudence Project
14		2.3 Feedback sessions	0.5 days	Thu 26/07/01	Prudence Project,Mary Dee
15		2.4 Consolidate results	1 day	Thu 26/07/01	Prudence Project
16		2.5 Finalise requirements	1 day	Fri 27/07/01	Prudence Project[50%],Bill Buggs[50%]
17		2.6 Evolve other recommendations	1 day	Mon 30/07/01	Prudence Project[50%],Bill Buggs
18		2.7 Carry out risk analysis	2 days	Tue 31/07/01	Prudence Project[50%]

5 Click the Filter down arrow on the Toolbar and select 'All Tasks'. The display returns to normal.

Resource Group...

All Tasks
Completed Tasks
Confirmed
Cost Greater Than...
Cost Overbudget
Created After...
Critical
Date Range...
In Progress Tasks
Incomplete Tasks
Late/Overbudget Tasks Assigned To...
Linked Fields

Printing Reports

This chapter covers the setup, preview and printing of charts and reports. It deals with headers and footers, scaling reports, previewing and printing. Finally it covers the Copy Picture facility which enables you to copy and paste from Project 2000 to another application (typically a word processor for preparing a project report).

Covers

Chapter Twelve

Printing

If your project is going to be successful you will need to communicate information on the project and its progress on a regular basis. In addition to the 26 pre-defined views (which you can print), Project 2000 also contains an additional 25 pre-defined report formats for printing information about your project.

Although the printed project Gantt chart is a very useful tool for communicating basic project progress information, different groups of people will need information presented to them in different ways.

The project team will need detailed information on the current stage, tasks and activities and their progress against schedule. They will also need to see the 'big picture' from time to time so that they don't lose sight of the overall project.

Management will usually only require information at the summary level together with details of what problems and issues have occurred, or perhaps might occur.

When faced with choices (such as 'do we increase the scope of the project to include this new area we have uncovered or do we stick with the original schedule?') you can produce reports that show the answers to the 'what if' type of questions.

The types of report that can be produced are as follows:

- Any chart view (using Print from the Toolbar).

- Overviews (summary, top-level and critical tasks).

- Current Activities (tasks due, in progress or slipping).

- Cost, Assignment, Workload or Custom reports.

The Page Setup dialogue box allows you to set the page orientation (portrait or landscape), adjust margin widths, change scales, create headers and footers and control the flow of information.

Headers and Footers

In addition to the basic information displayed in a report, Project 2000 allows you to create your own headers and footers which are displayed at the top and bottom of every page in a report. These are set up using the Page Setup dialogue box.

You can enter any text you like and also include any general system information (page number, date, title, etc.) and a wide range of project level information.

1 Open your project in Gantt Chart view and hide all subtasks.

2 Select File>Page Setup from the Menu bar (to open the Page Setup dialogue box) and click the Header tab.

3 Click the Center tab and then click in the text area below it.

4 Click the down arrow next to 'General', select 'Company Name' and click Add. Then repeat but select 'Project Title' and click Add.

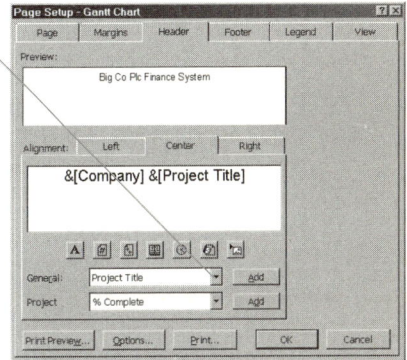

5 Now click the Footer tab and add 'Total Page Count' after the page number (put 'of' between them). Then click the Left Alignment tab, type 'Duration:', select Duration from the Project information drop down list (below the General list) and finally click OK to save the header and footer information.

Previewing Reports

With Project 2000 it is always a good idea to preview a report before printing it. That way you can make sure it will look the way you want, and make any final adjustments to it.

1 Open your project in Gantt Chart view with all subtasks hidden.

2 Click Print Preview on the Toolbar. Print Preview opens and looks something like this:

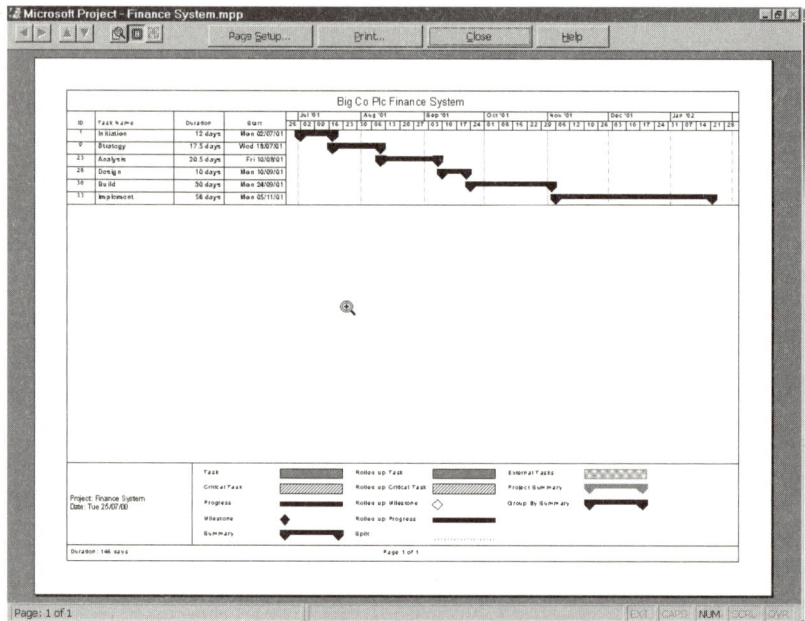

You can always print your current chart view using the Print button.

3 If you move your cursor over the Preview page it changes to a magnifying glass which allows you to zoom in and out.

4 Zoom in and check your header and footer information. (You can use Page Setup to change any details, such as the font size.) Click Close to exit Print Preview.

Print Setup and Scaling

In Project 2000 you can now set the paper size and many other details from the Page Setup dialogue box. You can also scale reports to get the best fit to a certain number of pages.

1   Open your project in Gantt Chart view, hide all subtasks and select File>Page Setup from the Menu bar. The Page Setup dialogue box opens:

2   Select the Page tab, select Fit to: 1 page wide by 1 page tall.

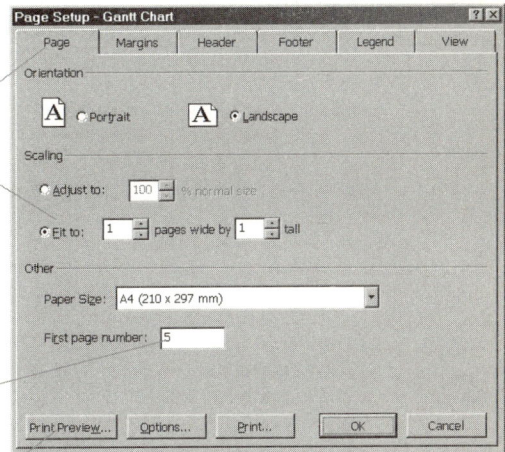

3   Click in 'First page number' and change it to 5.

4   Click 'Print Preview' to see how the print will look so far.

5   In the Print Preview screen click 'Page Setup' to reopen the Page Setup dialogue box. Then do the following:

   •   Select the Header tab and change the font size to 14 points.
   •   Select the Footer tab, change the font size to 12 points and delete the 'of &[Pages]' to get rid of the 'of 5' after the page number.

Click OK to see the revised Print Preview.

Printing Reports

There are 25 pre-defined report formats available in Project 2000, grouped into six categories.

1 Open your project in Gantt Chart view and view all subtasks. Select View>Reports from the Menu bar. The Reports dialogue box opens:

You can also just double-click on Current Activities.

2 Select 'Current Activities' and then click Select. The Current Activity Reports dialogue box opens:

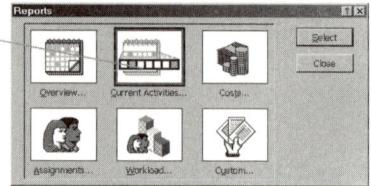

If you don't want to change the standard report, just click Select to preview and print it.

3 Select 'Unstarted Tasks' and then click Edit. The Task Report dialogue box opens:

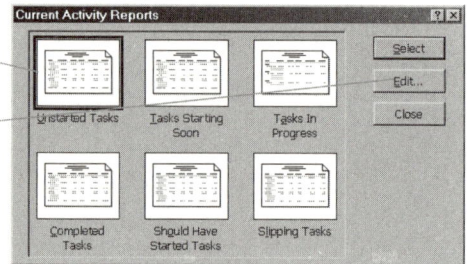

4 Select the Definition tab and select 'Show summary tasks'. Then select the Details tab (this is shown on the next page).

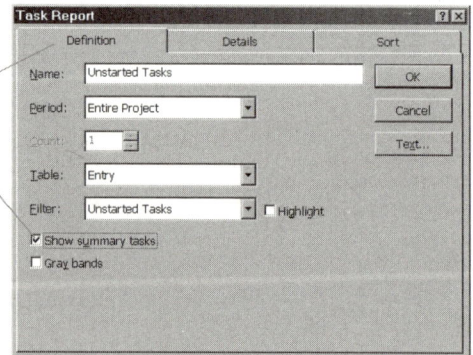

5 Select Assignment Notes in addition to Schedule and Task Notes. Select Gridlines between details. Click OK.

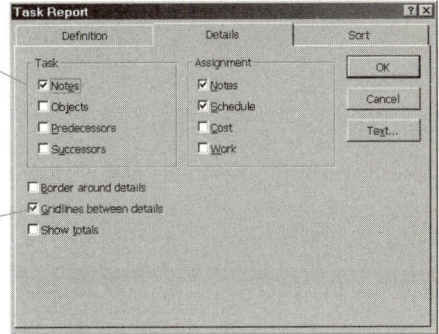

Project 2000 returns you to the Current Activity Reports dialogue box (as shown on the facing page).

6 Click Select in the Current Activity Reports dialogue box. The report is previewed:

Using these steps and Print Preview you can explore all the report formats available without needing to print.

7 Click Print and then OK to print the report. Finally click Cancel to close the Reports dialogue box.

Copy Picture

The Copy Picture facility in Project 2000 can be
selected from the Copy Picture button on the
Toolbar or through the Edit menu:

1 Open your project in Gantt Chart view and select
Show>Outline Level I from the Toolbar.

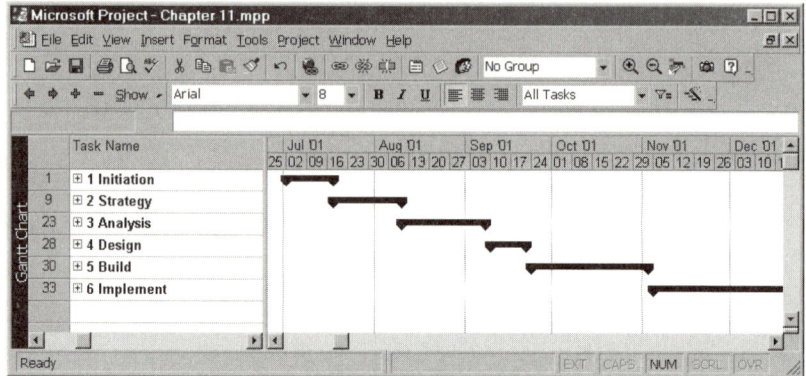

2 Adjust the panes to give approximately the required picture,
then click the Copy Picture button.

3 Under Timescale select
the From: and To:
options, enter the start
and end dates of your
project and click OK.

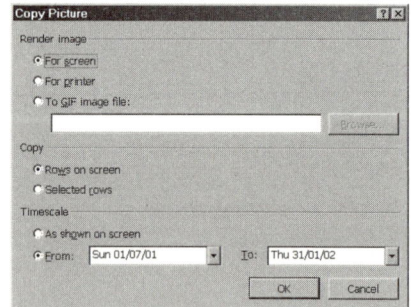

*If the picture is
large or will not
fit easily into
another
application,
Project 2000 will alert you.*

4 Open your target application (Word, etc.) and paste the
picture using Edit>Paste from the Menu bar.

Tracking Progress

This chapter introduces progress tracking and entering progress information. It explains the different types of progress information and how to deal with them.

Covers

Chapter Thirteen

Progress Tracking

Up to now you have been planning your project, allocating resources to it and then scheduling when things will happen. Once the project is actually under way you need to start tracking progress against your plan and schedule.

You enter information about progress by using actual start and completion dates as well as effort expended by resource.

If tasks are completed ahead of schedule you can then decide if you want to bring other tasks forward. If tasks are running late you can decide what actions you can take to help.

Again, the Gantt chart is the most effective way of tracking progress as it can show actual against the plan.

Before you begin to enter actual information, complete your plan in as much detail as you are able, using change budgets to allow for the unknown. Once you are happy with the plan you can set a baseline and then start progress tracking.

Project 2000 stores information under three headings:

Baseline: the plan dates which are compared with the actual and scheduled dates.

Actual: completed tasks or part-completed tasks.

Schedule: tasks that have not yet been started or work remaining on part-completed tasks.

The frequency with which you enter your information is up to you, but typically you would get progress details from the people working on the project at the end of each week.

As you enter your actual data the project is recalculated and rescheduled. So start at the earliest tasks on the schedule and work through. Once you have input all the actual information and seen the impact on the schedule you can re-evaluate the project and make any adjustments required to the project tasks to deal with issues that have arisen.

Progress Information

In addition to actual start and finish dates you can also input progress information on the percentage completed, actual and remaining duration, actual and remaining work and actual and remaining cost.

Depending on the type of information you input, Project 2000 will calculate the other relevant information.

If you input a task completion date, Project 2000 will set the actual start date to the scheduled start date and the actual duration to the difference between the start date and actual completion date.

The most accurate way of recording progress is to input the actual work done. This should be recorded by all the people resources you have working on the project. If this is less than the estimate for the task, Project 2000 will then calculate the work remaining as the difference between the actual work done and the original estimate.

While Project 2000's calculation of the work to completion may be acceptable at the beginning of a task, it is far more accurate to get people to record their own estimates of the work required to complete their tasks at the same time as they record the work done. You can then input this information and get a picture of the way the project is really going.

You can also input actual duration and, if that is less than the scheduled duration, Project 2000 calculates the remaining duration as the difference. If the task is actually completed in less than the scheduled duration, you need to set the remaining duration to zero. If it is going to be completed in less or more time you can again input your expected duration.

In the same way, you can enter actual and remaining costs.

You can input this task progress information in a number of views including Gantt Chart, Task Usage and Resource Usage views.

Completed Work

One a task has been completed, the easiest way to enter that information is simply by telling Project 2000 that the task is completed.

1 Open your project in Gantt Chart view and select Task 2 (Agree Project Objectives).

2 Select Tools>Tracking>Update Tasks from the Menu bar. The Update Tasks dialogue box appears:

3 Click the Finish date down arrow, select the scheduled finish date (02/07/01) and click OK.

After step 3, the task is completed and a tick is displayed in the Information field. The task is also removed from the Critical Path (it reverts to blue) and a progress bar (black line) is displayed through the task.

	ⓘ	Task Name	Duration	Start	02 Jul '01	09
					S M T W T F S S	M
1		⊟ 1 Initiation	12 days	Mon 02/07/01		
2	✓	1.1 Agree Project Objectives	1 day	Mon 02/07/01	▬ Prudence Project	
3	◆	1.2 Identify Stakeholders	1 day	Tue 03/07/01	Prudence Projec	
4		1.3 Identify Project Team	2 days	Wed 04/07/01	Bill Buggs[	

4 Select Tools>Tracking>Update Tasks from the Menu bar again. The actual start and finish dates are entered, the task is shown as 100% complete, the actual duration is shown as 1 day and the remaining duration is set to zero.

5 Click Cancel. Position the cursor over the task Information field. The date completed information pops up.

	ⓘ	Task Name	Duration
1		⊟ 1 Initiation	12 days
2	✓ ⊕	1.1 Agree Project Objectives	1 day
3	◆	✓ This task was completed on	1 day
4		Mon 02/07/01.	2 days

Part Completed Work

Where a number of hours or days of work have been carried out on a task but the task is not yet fully completed, you can enter the actual work carried out:

1 Open your project in Task Usage view and select Task 3 (Identify Stakeholders).

2 Select Format>Details>Actual Work from the Menu bar. The Actual Work fields are displayed underneath the estimated Work fields.

Click the Go To Selected Task button, if necessary, to bring the selected task into view.

	ⓘ	Task Name	Details	02 Jul 01		
				M	T	W
1		⊟ **Initiation**	Work	8h	8h	8h
			Act. Work	8h		
2	✓	⊟ Agree Project Objectives	Work	8h		
			Act. Work	8h		
		Prudence Project	Work	8h		
			Act. Work	8h		
3	◈	⊟ Identify Stakeholders	Work		8h	
			Act. Work			
		Prudence Project	Work		8h	
			Act. Work			

3 Click in the actual work field for the task.

4 Type '5' and press Enter. Accept any constraint warnings you may receive and continue.

	ⓘ	Task Name	Details	02 Jul 01		
				M	T	W
1		⊟ **Initiation**	Work	8h	5h	8h
			Act. Work	8h	5h	
2	✓	⊟ Agree Project Objectives	Work	8h		
			Act. Work	8h		
		Prudence Project	Work	8h		
			Act. Work	8h		
3	◈	⊟ Identify Stakeholders	Work		5h	3h
			Act. Work		5h	
	📊	Prudence Project	Work		5h	3h
			Act. Work		5h	

The actual hours are entered, the work is rescheduled from 8 to 5 hours and the remaining 3 hours are rescheduled for the following day.

Percentage Completed

There is a certain amount of risk involved in using percentage completed as the measure of work done on a task. It is human nature for most people to be optimistic about their progress so a measure of actual work done and estimate of work to completion is usually more accurate. However, it will sometimes be appropriate to use percentage completed where it's not practical to track work more closely.

1   Open your project in Task Sheet view (by selecting View>More Views>Task Sheet from the Menu bar and clicking Apply).

2   Select View>Table>Tracking from the Menu bar.

3   Select View>Toolbars>Tracking from the Menu bar.

If your tasks are still sorted from a previous topic, select Project>Sort> Sort By>Reset>Sort from the Toolbar.

4   Select Task 4 (Identify Project Team) and click the 75% Complete button on the Tracking Toolbar.

	Task Name	Act. Start	Act. Finish	% Comp.	Act. Dur.	Rem. Dur.	Act. Cost	Act. Work
1	⊟ Initiation	Mon 02/07/01	NA	38%	4.6 days	7.4 days	£620.00	25 hrs
2	Agree Project Objectives	Mon 02/07/01	Mon 02/07/01	100%	1 day	0 days	£160.00	8 hrs
3	Identify Stakeholders	Tue 03/07/01	NA	73%	1 day	0.38 days	£100.00	5 hrs
4	Identify Project Team	Wed 04/07/01	NA	75%	1.5 days	0.5 days	£360.00	12 hrs
5	Identify Business Case	NA	NA	0%	0 days	1 day	£0.00	0 hrs

You can input and adjust any percentage figure using the Update Tasks dialogue box.

The Actual Start date is entered as scheduled. The percentage completed is set to 75% and the Actual Duration, Remaining Duration, Actual Cost and Actual Work fields are all updated.

5   Select View>Gantt Chart from the Menu bar. The part completed tasks are shown with progress bars.

	ⓘ	Task Name	Duration	Start	02 Jul 01 S M T W T F S
1		⊟ 1 Initiation	12 days	Mon 02/07/01	
2	✓	1.1 Agree Project Objectives	1 day	Mon 02/07/01	Prudence Pro
3	◆	1.2 Identify Stakeholders	1.38 days	Tue 03/07/01	Prudence
4		1.3 Identify Project Team	2 days	Wed 04/07/01	Bill
5		1.4 Identify Business Case	1 day	Thu 05/07/01	

Duration Completed

In the same way as you can enter actual work done, you can also enter actual and remaining duration for a task.

1. Open your project in Gantt Chart view and select Task 6 (Analyse the Risks).

If you have the Tracking Toolbar displayed you can click the Update Tasks button.

2. Select Tools>Tracking>Update Tasks from the Menu bar. The Update Tasks dialogue box opens:

3. Click the Actual Duration up arrow to display 1 day then click OK. If you get a task scheduling conflict warning select 'Continue'. The task is updated on the Gantt Chart.

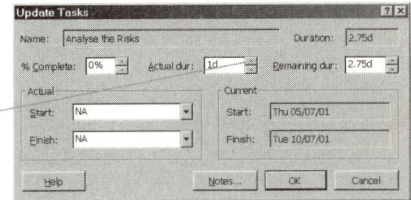

	ⓘ	Task Name	Duration	Start	02 Jul 01	09 Jul
					S M T W T F S S M T	
1		⊟ **1 Initiation**	**12 days**	**Mon 02/07/01**		
2	✓	1.1 Agree Project Objectives	1 day	Mon 02/07/01	Prudence Project	
3	◈	1.2 Identify Stakeholders	1.38 days	Tue 03/07/01	Prudence Project	
4		1.3 Identify Project Team	2 days	Wed 04/07/01	Bill Buggs[50	
5		1.4 Identify Business Case	1 day	Thu 05/07/01	Prud	
6		1.5 Analyse the Risks	2.75 days	Thu 05/07/01		
7	▣ ⌨	1.6 Produce Outline Project Plan	1 day	Tue 10/07/01		
8		1.7 Project Approval	0 days	Tue 17/07/01		

4. Select Tools> Tracking>Update Tasks again from the Menu bar. Note that the '% Complete' is set to 36%, 'Actual dur' to 1 day, 'Remaining dur' to 1.75d and 'Actual: Start' is set to the scheduled start date. Click Cancel and save your project file.

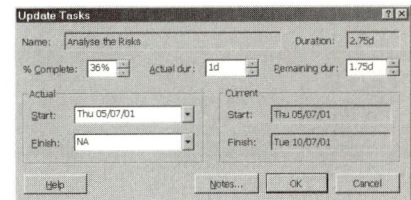

Entering Costs

Normally Project 2000 calculates actual costs for you based on the actual work and the cost details you have entered for the resource. However, you can also enter actual cost details directly:

1 Select Tools>Options from the Menu bar. The Options dialogue box opens:

2 Click the Calculation tab

3 Clear 'Actual costs are always calculated by Microsoft Project' and click OK.

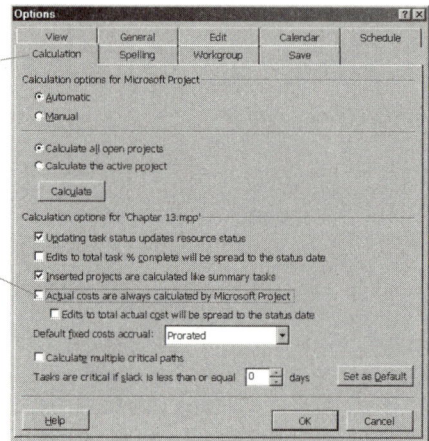

4 Select View>Task Usage from the Menu bar.

5 Select View>Table>Tracking from the Menu bar.

6 Select Format>Details>Actual Cost from the Menu bar.

You can only enter actual costs for completed tasks.

7 Click in Task 2, Actual Cost field. Type '200' and press Enter.

8 Close your file without saving it.

Updating as Scheduled

One or more tasks that have been started and/or completed as scheduled can be updated using the Update As Scheduled button on the Tracking Toolbar or the Update Project dialogue box.

1 Open your project in Gantt Chart view.

2 Select Tools>Tracking>Update Project to open the Update Project dialogue box:

3 Select 'Update work as completed through', set the date to 09/07/01 and click OK.

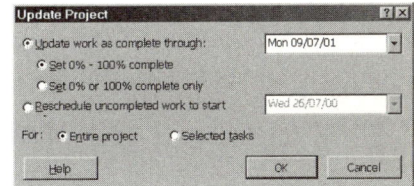

Update Project	? X
⊙ Update work as complete through:	Mon 09/07/01 ▾
⊙ Set 0% - 100% complete	
○ Set 0% or 100% complete only	
○ Reschedule uncompleted work to start	Wed 26/07/00 ▾
For: ⊙ Entire project ○ Selected tasks	
Help	OK Cancel

If you get a scheduling conflict warning select Continue and click OK. The tasks are now all shown as completed up to 9 July and Task 6 (Analyse the Risks) is shown as part completed up to 9 July.

	0	Task Name	Duration	Start	02 Jul 01							09 Jul 01			
---	---	---	---	---	S	M	T	W	T	F	S	S	M	T	W	T
1		⊟ 1 Initiation	12 days	Mon 02/07/01												
2	✓	1.1 Agree Project Objectives	1 day	Mon 02/07/01		Prudence Project										
3	✓	1.2 Identify Stakeholders	1.38 days	Tue 03/07/01			Prudence Project									
4	✓	1.3 Identify Project Team	2 days	Wed 04/07/01				Bill Buggs[50%],Pr								
5	✓	1.4 Identify Business Case	1 day	Thu 05/07/01						Prudence						
6		1.5 Analyse the Risks	2.75 days	Thu 05/07/01							Mary					
7	⊞ ✎	1.6 Produce Outline Project Plan	1 day	Tue 10/07/01											Prud	

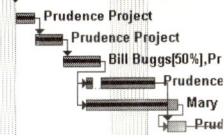

4 Select Task 6 (Analyse the Risks) and click the Update Tasks button on the Tracking Toolbar.

The task is shown at 77% completed with 2.13 days actual and 0.63 days remaining. Click Cancel.

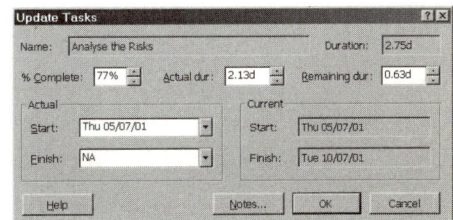

Update Tasks	? X
Name:	Analyse the Risks	Duration: 2.75d
% Complete: 77%	Actual dur: 2.13d	Remaining dur: 0.63d
Actual		**Current**
Start: Thu 05/07/01 ▾		Start: Thu 05/07/01
Finish: NA ▾		Finish: Tue 10/07/01
Help		Notes... OK Cancel

Actual v. Baseline

Having set the project baseline you can monitor your actual progress against the baseline at any time. The baseline and actual figures can be displayed in a number of Tables, through the use of Filters and in the Tracking Gantt Chart view.

1 In Gantt Chart view select Task 6 (Analyse the Risks) and click the Update Tasks button on the Tracking Toolbar. The Update Tasks dialogue box opens:

You can use the up and down arrows to step one day at a time.

2 Increase the Actual duration to 4 days, the Remaining duration to 1 day and click OK. You will probably receive a scheduling conflict warning. If so select 'Continue' and the project will be rescheduled.

3 Select View>Table>Work from the Menu bar and the Work Table view opens.
Note that 'Work' = 'Actual' + 'Remaining' and 'Variance' = 'Work' - 'Baseline'.

Use the Filter down arrow on the Toolbar to display over-budget or Slipping tasks.

	Task Name	Work	Baseline	Variance	Actual	Remaining
1	⊟ 1 Initiation	71.5 hrs	67 hrs	4.5 hrs	61.5 hrs	10 hrs
2	1.1 Agree Project Objectives	8 hrs	8 hrs	0 hrs	8 hrs	0 hrs
3	1.2 Identify Stakeholders	8 hrs	8 hrs	0 hrs	8 hrs	0 hrs
4	1.3 Identify Project Team	16 hrs	16 hrs	0 hrs	16 hrs	0 hrs
5	1.4 Identify Business Case	16 hrs	16 hrs	0 hrs	16 hrs	0 hrs
6	1.5 Analyse the Risks	15.5 hrs	11 hrs	4.5 hrs	13.5 hrs	2 hrs
7	1.6 Produce Outline Project Plan	8 hrs	8 hrs	0 hrs	0 hrs	8 hrs
8	1.7 Project Approval	0 hrs	0 hrs	0 hrs	0 hrs	0 hrs

4 Select View>Table>Cost to see the Actual and Baseline cost, and View>Table>Variance to see the start and finish date variance from Baseline.

Tracking Gantt Chart

The Tracking Gantt Chart gives a graphical representation of the actual state of the project compared to the baseline.

1 Select View > Tracking Gantt from the Menu bar and adjust your view so that it looks like the following:

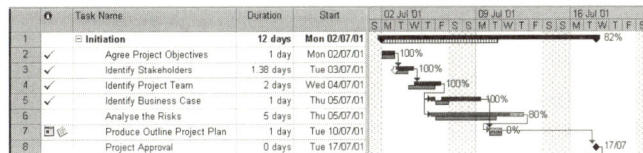

Note the following:

- Actual progress is shown as a hatched line underneath summary Task 1 (Initiation).

- The baseline is shown in grey beneath the actual and scheduled task bars.

- For Task 2 (Agree Project Objectives) the actual and baseline are the same as the task was completed to schedule.

- Task 3 (Identify Stakeholders) started on schedule but was completed 0.38 days late.

- Tasks 4 and 5 were completed to their estimated duration but were started late (due to Task 3) and therefore finished late.

- Task 6 started early but will be finished late so Task 7 should also start and finish late (but with a constraint).

- Finally, there is no baseline milestone (an empty diamond) as the scheduled milestone (a solid diamond) is also the baseline (i.e. it is still on schedule).

Having some lag time in your schedule allows you to cope with task delays without throwing out the whole schedule.

2 Double-click on Task 7 and remove the constraint (as soon as possible). Now the milestone has slipped, so reduce the lag time to 2 days to bring it back on schedule again.

Project Statistics

The Project Statistics dialogue box gives you summary level information for the whole project:

1 Select Project > Project Information from the Menu bar. The Project Information dialogue box opens:

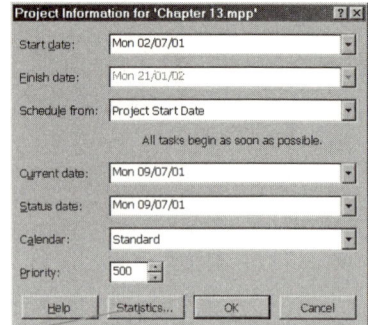

2 Click Statistics. The Project Statistics dialogue box opens:

Project Information for 'Chapter 13.mpp'

Start date:	Mon 02/07/01
Finish date:	Mon 21/01/02
Schedule from:	Project Start Date
	All tasks begin as soon as possible.
Current date:	Mon 09/07/01
Status date:	Mon 09/07/01
Calendar:	Standard
Priority:	500

Help   Statistics...   OK   Cancel

Project Statistics for 'Chapter 13.mpp'

	Start	Finish
Current	Mon 02/07/01	Mon 21/01/02
Baseline	Mon 02/07/01	Mon 21/01/02
Actual	Mon 02/07/01	NA
Variance	0d	0d

	Duration	Work	Cost
Current	146d	735.5h	£36,132.50
Baseline	146d	731h	£36,065.00
Actual	13.57d	61.5h	£1,402.50
Remaining	132.43d	674h	£34,730.00

Percent complete:
Duration: 9%   Work: 8%

Close

The top section shows the current, baseline, actual and variance for the start and finish dates.

The middle section shows statistics on the duration, work and cost of the project.

Note that despite some of the tasks in Stage 1 (Initiation) running late we have kept the project on schedule by reducing the lag time. However, we are currently over budget on the Work and Cost.

The final section shows the overall percentage completed in Duration and Work.

Progress Lines

Progress Lines can be drawn on the Gantt Chart or Tracking Gantt Chart at any date to show the actual or expected progress at that date.

They work by linking the tasks that are scheduled to be started, completed or in progress on that date. Tasks that are behind schedule result in peaks to the left of the line, and tasks that are ahead of schedule result in peaks to the right of the line.

1 Open your project in Gantt Chart view and make sure the Tracking Toolbar is displayed.

2 Click the Add Progress Line button on the Tracking Toolbar. The cursor changes to a jagged line with an arrow either side.

3 Move the cursor over the Gantt Chart until the pop-up box displays a Progress Date of 13 July.

	Progress Line	
Progress Date:		Fri 13/07/01
	Click the mouse to display a progress line on this date	

4 Click on that date and the progress line will be displayed on the chart.

	❶	Task Name	Duration	Start	02 Jul 01	09 Jul 01
					S M T W T F S S	M T W T F S S
1		⊟ 1 Initiation	11.88 days	Mon 02/07/01		
2	✓	1.1 Agree Project Objectives	1 day	Mon 02/07/01	Prudence Project	
3	✓	1.2 Identify Stakeholders	1.38 days	Tue 03/07/01	Prudence Project	
4	✓	1.3 Identify Project Team	2 days	Wed 04/07/01	Bill Buggs[50%],Prudence P	
5	✓	1.4 Identify Business Case	1 day	Thu 05/07/01	Prudence Project,	
6		1.5 Analyse the Risks	5 days	Thu 05/07/01	Mary De	
7	✎	1.6 Produce Outline Project Plan	1 day	Thu 12/07/01	Prude	
8		1.7 Project Approval	0 days	Tue 17/07/01		

You can place multiple progress lines on a chart and delete any of them in the Progress Lines dialogue box.

5 To remove a progress line, double-click the line and the Progress Lines dialogue box opens. Click Delete then click OK and the progress line is removed.

When is a Task Completed?

This chapter has concentrated on tracking progress of your project by entering details of tasks and work completed. But one of the difficult decisions facing a project manager is exactly when do you treat a task as completed?

The old quotation used to be 'The job's not over until the paperwork's done.' Usually accompanied by a picture of a small child on a potty!

The more formal answer is that the task has been completed when everything that needs to be done has been done. If the task was to produce something tangible like a report or specification then the task is not completed until the product has been produced and formally signed off. This should include any quality control or management approval.

Experienced project managers will be aware of the 80% completed syndrome. This is a reflection of peoples' basic optimism when estimating the work remaining to complete a task. This is the reason why using percentage completed figures is not usually very accurate.

So to be realistic, use the actual work effort used and the estimated work to completion. In the early stages of a task these should add up to the work estimated for the task. As the task progresses they should begin to show if the task is going to take more or less work than the original estimate. And there should be no sudden last minute surprises.

The job's not over until the paperwork's done!

If someone is estimating that they will be completing a task to plan until the very last moment and then it suddenly increases, they were not being realistic. As the project manager you should feed that back to them (in a constructive way) so that they will hopefully be more accurate in future tasks.

Finally, if they have used up all the estimated time and the task is still not formally completed or signed off, then they should still be showing some work as their estimate to completion.

Customising

This chapter introduces the customising of tables, views, reports and fields in Project 2000. It also shows you how to share customised items between projects.

Covers

Chapter Fourteen

Customising Project 2000

Project 2000 has a large number of pre-defined tables, views, reports and fields. These will probably cover most requirements for most projects. However, if you do need a different table, view, report or field, Project 2000 allows you to customise or create new ones. In addition to being able to change the sequence of columns in a table, view or report, there are over 200 different fields holding information that you can access and custom fields that you can use for any other information.

Tables

Tables are made up of columns and rows of information and there are 29 pre-defined task and resource tables available in Project 2000. If none of these match your requirements you can create your own custom tables to include exactly the information you require. You can also combine your custom tables with pre-defined or custom filters.

Views

Project 2000 contains 26 pre-defined views which display schedule information and allow you to edit it. Some of these views are single views and some are combination views. Single views consist of a screen, table and filter. Combination views combine two single views on the same screen by splitting them one above the other. Custom views can be based on any combination.

Reports

Project 2000 contains 25 pre-defined reports split into five report groups. Custom reports can be based on any of these existing reports or they can be created completely from new. If you create a new report it can be based on one of four report templates: Task Report, Resource Report, Monthly Calendar Report and Crosstab Report.

Fields

Project 2000 contains the facility for 130 custom fields which you can use to hold additional information, carry out calculations or hold graphical indicators.

Custom Tables

Custom tables can be created from new but it is usually easier to copy an existing table and then edit it.

1 Open your project in Gantt Chart view, select View > Table > More Tables > Summary from the Menu bar, then click Copy. The Table Definition dialogue box opens with a copy of the Summary table displayed.

2 Type 'Project Summary Table' in the Name.

3 In the Field Name column select Duration and click Delete Row. The row is deleted from the definitions. Now delete Finish and Cost in the same way.

4 Now select %Complete and click Insert Row. Click the down arrow, select Actual Start and press Tab. The default values are inserted for the other fields. Now insert Actual Work in front of %Complete.

You can also press Enter or select another field to insert the default values.

5 Select Work and click Cut Row. Select Actual Work and click Paste Row.

Table Definition in 'Project1.mpp'

Name: Project Summary Table   ☐ Show in menu

Table

| Cut Row | Copy Row | Paste Row | Insert Row | Delete Row |

Field Name	Align Data	Width	Title	Align Title
ID	Center	5		Center
Name	Left	24	Task Name	Left
Start	Right	12		Center
Actual Start	Right	10		Center
Work	Right	10		Center
Actual Work	Right	10		Center
% Complete	Right	9	% Comp.	Center

Date format: Default   Row height: 1

☑ Lock first column   OK   Cancel

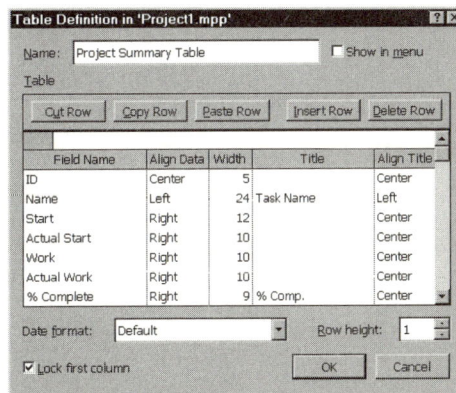

6 Click OK and then click Apply. The new table is applied to your Gantt Chart view.

Custom Views

Custom views can be created as single views or as combination views. First we will create a new single view:

1. Open your project, select View>More Views from the Menu bar and click New. The Define New View dialogue box opens:

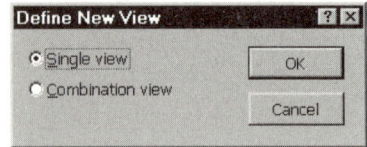

Define New View

- ● Single view
- ○ Combination view

OK   Cancel

2. Make sure Single view is selected and click OK. The View Definition dialogue box opens:

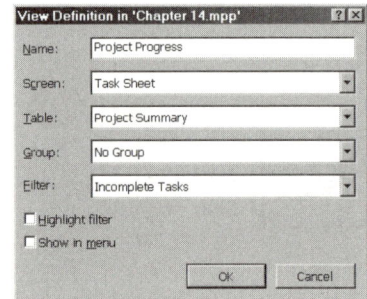

3. Type the name 'Project Progress', select 'Task Sheet', 'Project Summary Table', 'No Group', 'Incomplete Tasks' and click OK. The More Views box is displayed again.

View Definition in 'Chapter 14.mpp'

Name:	Project Progress
Screen:	Task Sheet
Table:	Project Summary
Group:	No Group
Filter:	Incomplete Tasks

☐ Highlight filter
☐ Show in menu

OK   Cancel

4. Make sure that 'Project Progress' is selected and click Apply. The new Project Progress single view is displayed with all incomplete tasks (tasks that are in progress or not yet started) displayed:

	Task Name	Start	Actual Start	Work	Actual Work	% Comp.
1	⊟ **Initiation**	**Mon 02/07/01**	**Mon 02/07/01**	**71.5 hrs**	**61.5 hrs**	**82%**
6	Analyse the Risks	Thu 05/07/01	Thu 05/07/01	15.5 hrs	13.5 hrs	80%
7	Produce Outline Project Plan	Thu 12/07/01	NA	8 hrs	0 hrs	0%
8	Project Approval	Tue 17/07/01	NA	0 hrs	0 hrs	0%
9	⊟ **Strategy**	**Tue 17/07/01**	**NA**	**104 hrs**	**0 hrs**	**0%**
10	⊟ **Carry out interviews**	**Tue 17/07/01**	**NA**	**32 hrs**	**0 hrs**	**0%**
11	Interview Managers	Tue 17/07/01	NA	16 hrs	0 hrs	0%
12	Interview Staff	Wed 18/07/01	NA	16 hrs	0 hrs	0%
13	Produce draft requirements	Mon 23/07/01	NA	16 hrs	0 hrs	0%
14	Feedback sessions	Wed 25/07/01	NA	8 hrs	0 hrs	0%
15	Consolidate results	Thu 26/07/01	NA	8 hrs	0 hrs	0%
16	Finalise requirements	Fri 27/07/01	NA	8 hrs	0 hrs	0%
17	Evolve other recommendations	Mon 30/07/01	NA	12 hrs	0 hrs	0%
18	Carry out risk analysis	Tue 31/07/01	NA	8 hrs	0 hrs	0%
19	Produce forward plan	Thu 02/08/01	NA	4 hrs	0 hrs	0%
20	⊟ **Report to management**	**Fri 03/08/01**	**NA**	**8 hrs**	**0 hrs**	**0%**

Combination View

To create a combination view we can use our new custom view and combine it with another view:

1 Select View > More Views from the Menu bar and click New.

2 Select Combination view and click OK.

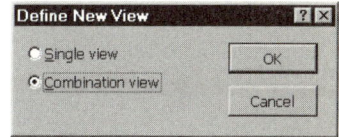

3 Type the name 'Progress Review', select 'Detail Gantt' for the Top and 'Project Progress' for the Bottom, click OK and then click Apply in More Views. The new combination view is displayed:

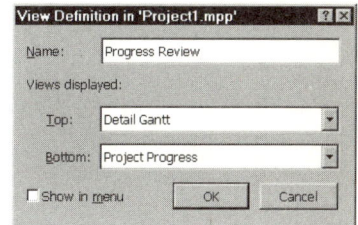

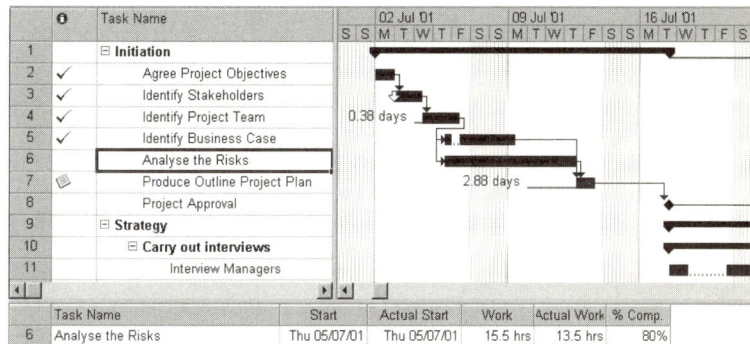

4 Move up and down the tasks in the top pane and the relevant task progress details are displayed in the bottom pane.

5 To display details of several tasks in the bottom pane select multiple tasks by dragging across them in the top pane.

Custom Reports

While you can always produce a custom report by starting with an existing report which is close to your requirements and then customising it, you may sometimes want to produce a completely new report.

1 Select View > Reports > Custom and click Select. The Custom Reports dialogue box opens:

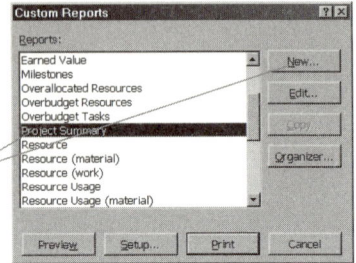

2 Select 'Project Summary' (note that the Copy button is not selectable) and click New. The Define New Report dialogue box opens:

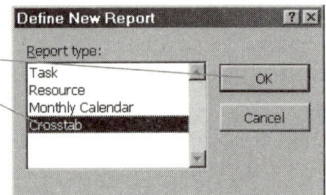

3 Select 'Crosstab' and click OK. The Crosstab Report dialogue box opens:

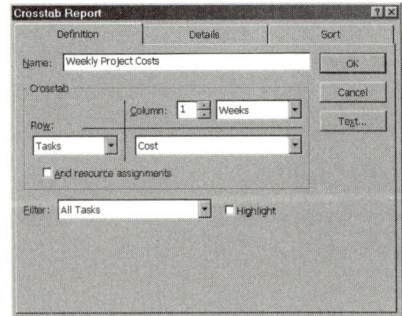

4 Select the Definition tab. Type the name 'Weekly Project Costs'. Under 'Row' select 'Tasks' and 'Cost'.

5 Select the Details tab (this is shown at the top of the facing page).

6 On the Details tab select 'Column totals' and click OK. The Custom Reports dialogue box is displayed:

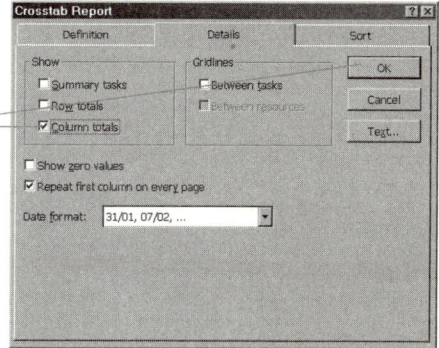

7 Select 'Weekly Project Costs' and click Preview. Your report should look something like the following:

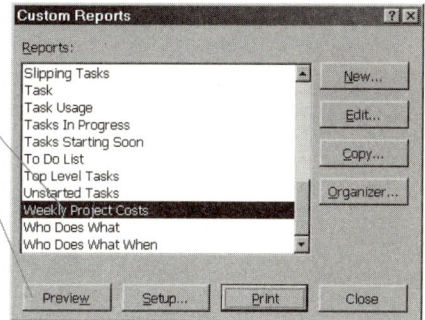

Weekly Project Costs as of Mon 02/07/01
Finance System

	02/07	09/07	16/07	23/07	30/07	06/08
Agree Project Objectives	£160.00					
Identify Stakeholders	£160.00					
Identify Project Team	£480.00					
Identify Business Case	£300.00	£100.00				
Analyse the Risks	£94.50	£198.00				
Produce Outline Project Plan		£160.00				
Project Approval						
Interview Managers			£160.00	£140.00		
Interview Staff		£320.00				
Produce draft requirements				£320.00		
Feedback sessions				£140.00		
Consolidate results				£160.00		
Finalise requirements				£150.00	£90.00	
Evolve other recommendations					£400.00	
Carry out risk analysis					£160.00	
Produce forward plan					£80.00	
Prepare Report					£50.00	£70.00
Present to Management						£40.00
Agree Requirements						£40.00
Select Package						
Purchase Package						
Change Budget						
Change Budget						
Install Package						
Change Budget						
Train Users						
Convert to New Package						
Change Budget						
Total	£1,134.50	£458.00	£500.00	£910.00	£780.00	£150.00

Custom Fields

While previous versions of Project have allowed you to store custom information, Project 2000 now enables you to manipulate that data, set up lists of acceptable values (value lists) to make data entry more accurate, set formulae to perform calculations on the data and set graphic indicators to represent data.

1   To work with custom fields select Tools>Customise>Fields from the Menu bar.
The Customise Fields dialogue box opens:

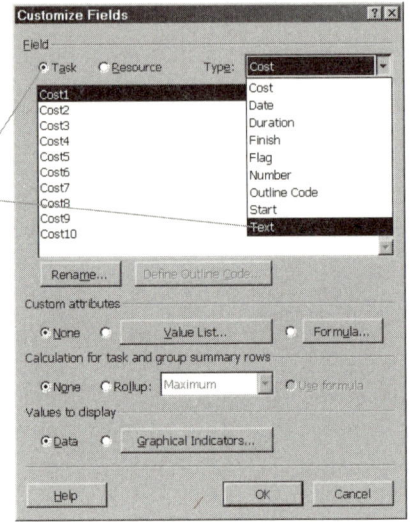

2   To associate a risk level with each task we will use a custom field, so select 'Task' and 'Text' (note the other field types available).

3   Select 'Text 1' from the list and click 'Rename'. The Rename Field dialogue box opens:

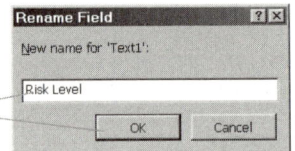

4   Type 'Risk Level' and click OK.

> *You can also set formulae in a custom field. These can operate on any Project 2000 fields and utilise native Visual Basic functions. The formula syntax is the same as for Microsoft Access.*
>
> *See 'Access 2000 in easy steps' for more information.*

Custom Fields: Value Lists

5   Now click the 'Value List' button as we need to pre-define a list of acceptable values for the field. The Value List dialogue box opens (shown at top of the facing page).

6 Type in the Values shown (High, Medium, Low and No Risk).

7 Select 'Use a value from the list…', select 'No Risk' and click the Set Default button. You will receive a warning that existing data may be invalidated. Click OK.

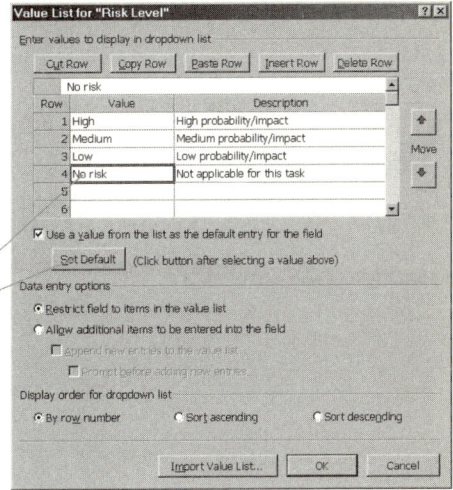

8 To use our new custom field we need to create a new table. In Gantt Chart view select View>Table>More Tables>Copy from the Toolbar. The Table Definition dialogue box opens. Type 'Risk Management' in the Name, select field name 'Duration' and change it to Text 1 (Risk Level), Align Data 'Left', Width '7' and Title 'Risk'. Click OK and click Apply. The new Risk column is displayed.

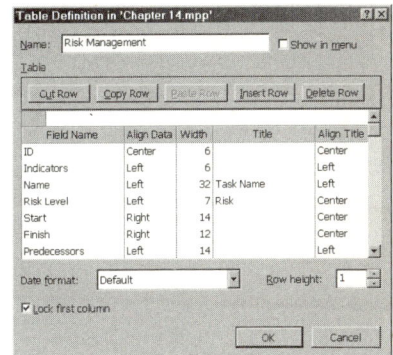

9 Select some of the incomplete tasks and apply risk levels to them (Low, Medium, High or No risk).

Graphic Indicators

Graphical indicators (traffic lights as they are sometimes called) are small coloured images that can be assigned to display in custom fields based on the value in the field, a value list selection or a formula calculation result.

You need to have completed the previous topic before this one.

1 Open your project in Gantt Chart view and select View>Tables>More Tables>Risk Management. Click Apply to get the risks into view. It should be like the following:

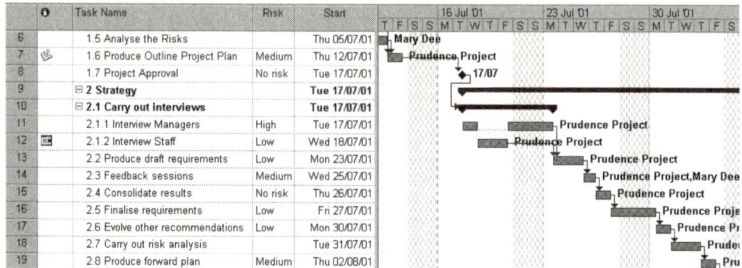

2 Select Tools>Customise>Fields>Risk Level from the Toolbar and click the Graphic Indicators button.

3 In the Graphic Indicators dialogue box select (Test) 'equals', (Value) 'High' and (Image) the red circle. Then do the same for the other values using yellow, green and white circles. Click OK and OK again.

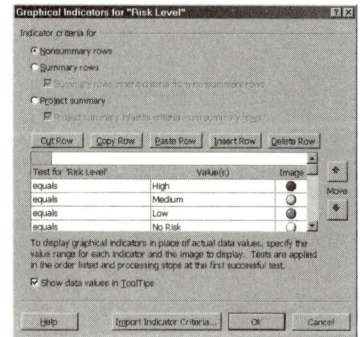

You can change things like reducing the width of the column and centring it by double-clicking the column header.

Your risks should now be shown as traffic lights similar to the illustration here:

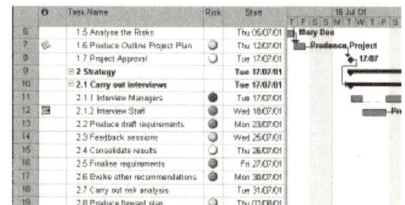

Sharing Custom Items

Any custom tables, views, reports, fields, value lists or formulae that you create in Project 2000 are stored in the host project file. However, you can make these items available to other projects by using the Organizer.

1 Open your project file and click the New button on the Toolbar. A new blank project is created and the Project Information dialogue box opens.

2 Click Cancel, then select File>Save As from the Menu bar and save the file as 'Share Test'.

3 Select View>Table>More Tables from the Menu bar and click Organizer. The Organizer dialogue box opens at the Tables tab.

4 In the 'Tables available in' field, select your project.

5 Select Risk Management and click Copy. The Risk Management Table is copied to the new file.

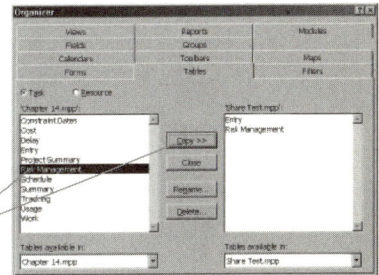

6 Click Close and the More Tables dialogue box is displayed.

7 Select Risk Management and click Apply. The Risk Management Table is applied to the view.

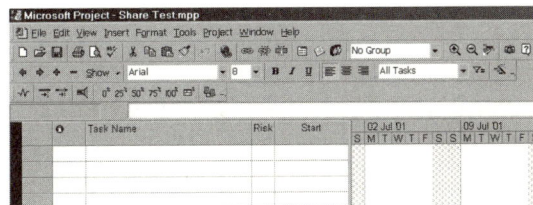

A Word of Caution

Although Project 2000 allows you to customise and change just about every table, view and report, it is good practice to use a copy of a pre-defined item and not change the pre-defined items themselves.

That way if you make a mistake you can just delete the new item and start again.

Murphy has a word of caution as well:

> # Murphy's 2nd Law
>
> Anything you try to change will take much longer and cost much more than you thought

Murphy's Second Law applies to just about everything and projects in particular. If your project involves computers or channel tunnels it is widely believed that the impact of Murphy's Second Law doubles!

On the subject of Murphy, here's another relevant one:

> # Murphy's 3rd Law
>
> If everything seems to be going well, you obviously don't know what's going on

Hyperlinks and the Web

This chapter explains hyperlinks and how to create them. It goes on to cover the creation of HTML and GIF files for publishing on the Web, and finally creating an export map.

Covers

Chapter Fifteen

Using Hyperlinks

Hyperlinks (hypertext links) were developed on the World Wide Web and provide a simple way of jumping from inside one document to another document. With a hyperlink you can jump to another document on your own computer, your local area network or another document anywhere on the Web (if you have an Internet connection).

With a hyperlink you can even open the document you are linking to at any particular point that has a reference.

When inserting a hyperlink, always check that the destination document exists!

To follow a hyperlink you just click on it. Pausing your cursor over a hyperlink will usually display some information about it, such as its address in the form of a Uniform Resource Locator (URL), i.e.:

http://www.ineasysteps.com

In Project 2000 you can create a hyperlink to another document on any task, resource or assignment using the Insert Hyperlink button.

The hyperlink symbol is displayed in the Indicators field and the hyperlink details are stored in the Hyperlink field. You can also insert a hyperlink in a text column on a sheet view.

Documents published on the World Wide Web are written in a language called HyperText Markup Language (HTML) which is read and interpreted by a program called a Web Browser. Microsoft Internet Explorer is one of the most widely used Task browsers. If you have a Task browser on your computer, clicking on a hypertext link to a HTML document in Project 2000 will open your browser and then open the HTML document in it. Closing it will return you to Project 2000.

If the hypertext link is to a Word or Excel document on your computer or network, Project 2000 will open Word or Excel and then open the document in that program. Closing it will return you to Project 2000.

Inserting a Hyperlink

Adding a hypertext link to a project is very straightforward:

1 Create the following simple HTML file using a text editor:

```
<html>
<head>
<title>Simple HTML File</title>
</head>
<body>
A simple HTML file.
</body>
</html>
```

Save the file with a .htm extension.

You can use Windows Notepad as your text editor.

2 Open your project in Gantt Chart view, select Task 6 (Analyse the Risks) and click the Insert Hyperlink button on the Toolbar.
The Insert Hyperlink dialogue box opens:

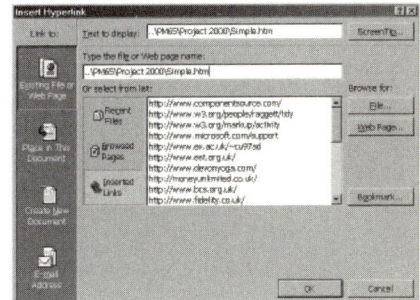

3 Click Browse, locate your HTML file and click OK. The hypertext symbol is inserted in the Indicator field.

If you don't have a Web Browser, create a link to a Word document or another type of file.

4 Pause your cursor over the hypertext symbol. The cursor changes to a pointing finger and the file name pops up:

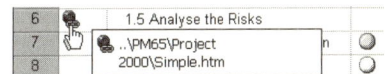

6		1.5 Analyse the Risks		
7		..\PM65\Project	n	
8		2000\Simple.htm		

5 Click on the link to jump to the file. Your browser opens and displays the file. Click Back (or close the browser) to return.

Publishing to HTML

With Project 2000, Microsoft have also introduced Project Central (a companion product) which has far more options for Web publishing and exchanging information.

Project data can be saved from Project 2000 in HTML format for publishing as Web pages on the Internet or on an internal Intranet. While you cannot save the entire project as an HTML file, you can save data from it.

Data is saved using import/export maps which determine which fields of data will be exported.

You may need to expand the Save menu to find 'Save as Web Page'.

1 Open your project and select File>Save As Web Page from the Menu bar. The File Save dialogue box opens.

2 Select the directory where you want to export the file to, type in a file name and click the Save button. The Export Mapping dialogue box opens.

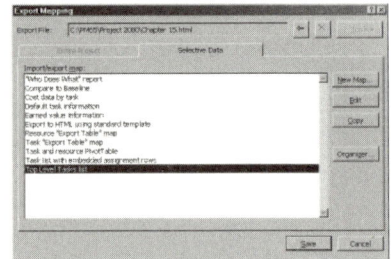

3 Select 'Top Level Tasks list' and click Save. The file is saved into your selected directory.

4 View the file in your Web Browser:

Finance System

Project Start Date: Mon 02/07/01
Project Finish Date: Mon 21/01/02

Top Level Tasks

ID	Task Name	Duration	Start	Finish	% Complete	Cost	Work
1	Initiation	11.88 days	Mon 02/07/01	Tue 17/07/01	82%	£1,592.50	71.5 hrs
9	Strategy	17.63 days	Tue 17/07/01	Fri 10/08/01	0%	£2,300.00	104 hrs
23	Analysis	20.5 days	Fri 10/08/01	Fri 07/09/01	0%	£21,680.00	80 hrs
28	Design	10 days	Mon 10/09/01	Fri 21/09/01	0%	£1,760.00	80 hrs
30	Build	30 days	Mon 24/09/01	Fri 02/11/01	0%	£5,280.00	240 hrs
33	Implement	56 days	Mon 05/11/01	Mon 21/01/02	0%	£3,520.00	160 hrs

Copying to GIF Files

Although export maps are useful and can be edited, you can only export data to HTML files. If you want to export a picture like a Gantt Chart you need to export it as a GIF (Graphic Image Format) file.

This is done through the Copy Picture facility:

1 Open your project in Gantt Chart view.

2 Click the Copy Picture button on the Toolbar. The Copy Picture dialogue box opens:

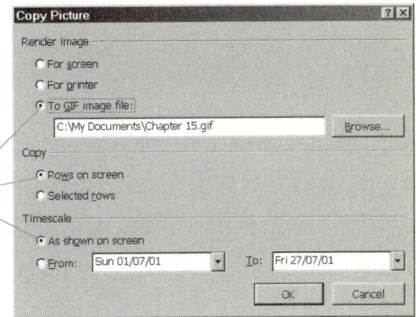

3 Select To GIF Image file, Rows on screen, As shown on screen, and click OK.

4 Now view the GIF file using your Task browser or other suitable utility. It should look like the following:

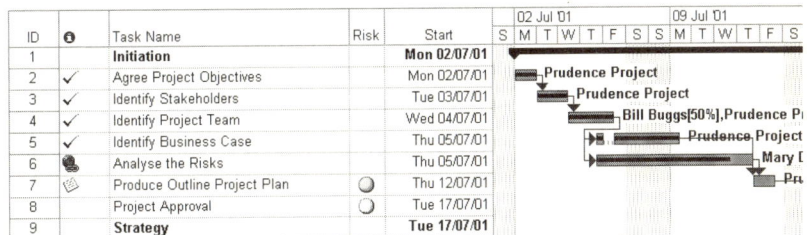

Once you have created a GIF file of the image you want to use, you can include it in an export map. This is covered in the next topic.

Export Maps

You could try out some of the other export maps such as 'Export to HTML using standard template' which lists the tasks, resources and assignments.

In addition to the pre-defined export maps you can also edit existing export maps or define new ones.

1 Select File > Save As Web Page from the Menu bar and click Save. The Export Mapping dialogue box opens.

2 Click New Map. The Define Import/Export Map dialogue box opens.

3 Type the name 'Test Map', select Include image file in HTML page and select the GIF file created in the last topic.

4 Click Data to import/export Tasks. The Task Mapping tab becomes active.

5 Click in the From field and select ID, Name, Start, Work and Cost. Click OK. The Export Mapping dialogue box is displayed.

Typing the first couple of characters of a field name usually brings it up.

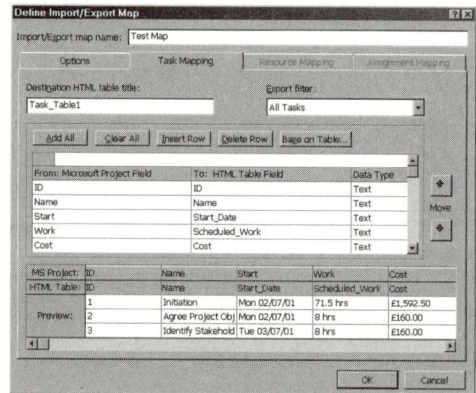

6 Select 'Test Map' and click Save. The HTML file is saved.

7 View the HTML file using your Web browser. The Gantt Chart is displayed as a graphic image followed by your data in a table.

Network Diagrams

This chapter explains what Network Diagrams (formerly PERT Charts) are and how to use them. It shows you how to add nodes, change dependencies and format the chart.

Covers

Chapter Sixteen

Network Diagrams

Network Diagrams were known in previous versions of Project as PERT Charts and are also sometimes referred to as Activity Diagrams. They give you a graphical view of tasks and dependencies. Each task is shown as a box (called a node) which can display up to five fields. The default fields are Task Name, Task ID, Scheduled Duration, Scheduled Start Date and Scheduled Finish Date. The lines linking the tasks reflect the task dependencies.

The shape of each node denotes the level or type of task:

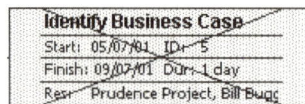

Completed Task

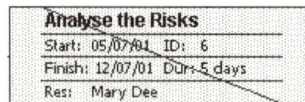

Started Task (not yet completed)

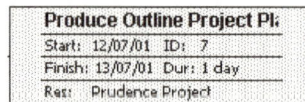

Unstarted Task

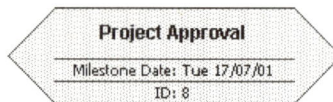

Milestone

Summary Task

Summary tasks can be expanded or contracted to show or hide subtasks by clicking on the + or - symbols.

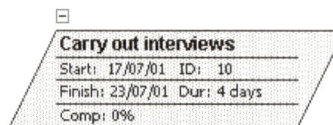

Tasks on the Critical Path are shown in red, tasks not on the Critical Path are shown in blue and filtered tasks are shown in yellow.

The Network Diagram provides a different type of view of the project from the Gantt Chart but any changes made in either are reflected in the project and the other views.

Network Diagram View

Although Network Diagrams are no longer as popular as they once were (having been largely replaced by the Gantt Chart) they still provide a useful alternate view of a project.

1 Open your project in Gantt Chart view and select Task 6 (Analyse the Risks).

2 Select View>Network Diagram from the Menu bar. The Network Diagram is displayed with Task 6 selected.

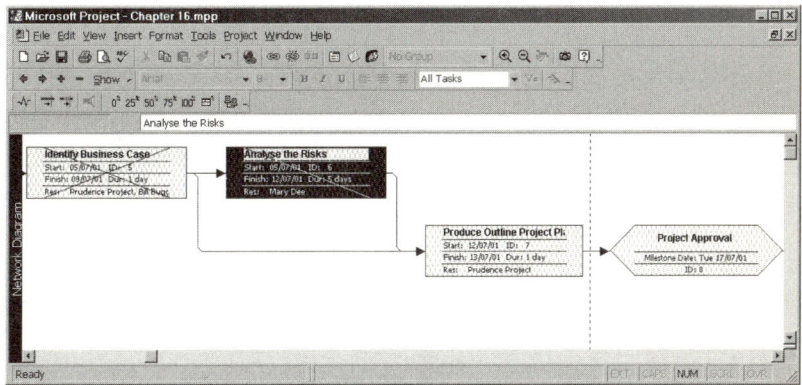

3 Use the Zoom In and Zoom Out buttons on the Toolbar together with the scrollbars to move around the Network Diagram. Note that you cannot zoom in to more than 400% or out to less than 25%.

4 Find Task 15 (Consolidate Results), select it by clicking on it and select View>Tracking Gantt from the Menu bar. Note that Task 15 is also selected in the Tracking Gantt. Click on the Go To Selected Task button on the Toolbar to bring the task into view on the Gantt Chart. (Moving between Network Diagram view and Gantt Chart view is very simple.)

Adding a Node

As well as being able to amend task details in Network Diagram view, you can also add a node (task) to the chart.

When you inserted a task in Gantt Chart view, it was inserted in front of the selected task. In Network Diagram view a new task is inserted after the selected task.

HOT TIP

The F5 key is a shortcut to Go to a Task.

1 Open your project in Network Diagram view and select Task 24 (Agree Requirements) by pressing F5, typing '24' and then pressing Enter. Task 24 is selected and positioned in the view.

HOT TIP

Your box will be re-sized to the same size as the other nodes.

2 Position your cursor below Task 24, then drag it to create a box. A new Task 25 is inserted with the Name field selected (the other tasks are renumbered from 26).

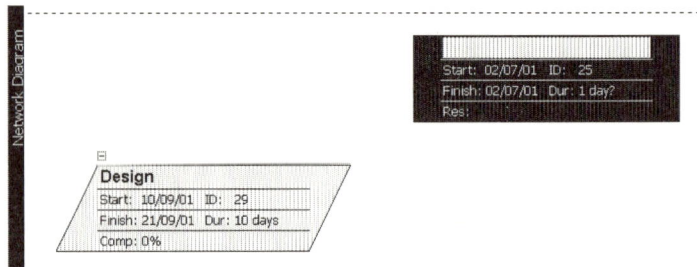

HOT TIP

If you position your cursor above a node, the node will expand so that you can see the information in it more clearly.

3 Type 'Issue Requirements' and press Enter.
The duration is automatically set to the default of 1 day.

4 Select Task 28 (Change Budget), click in the Duration field, type '2' and press Enter (this reduces the Change Budget to keep the overall total the same).

5 Save your project file.

As you identify and add tasks to the later stages of a project you should reduce your contingency figure accordingly to keep the overall duration constant.

Changing Dependencies

Once you have added a new node or task you will normally need to make changes to the dependencies to incorporate it.

In Network Diagram view you select existing dependencies by double-clicking on the linking lines. To create a new dependency you drag from the preceding task to the dependant task. By default a finish-to-start dependency is created. You can then double-click on the line to make any changes.

If the task you want to connect to is out of the view drag to the left margin and the diagram will scroll.

1 Zoom out and place your cursor on Task 24 (Agree requirements) and drag down to Task 25 (Issue Requirements). When you release the mouse button the dependency is created and the new node moved into position.

2 Now create a dependency from Task 25 (Issue Requirements) to Task 26 (Select Package). The dependency between Task 24 and Task 26 is now a redundant dependency (as it is implied by the new dependencies you have inserted).

3 Double-click on the dependency line between Task 24 and Task 26 and the Task Dependency pop-up box opens. Click Delete. (The redundant dependency is removed and the nodes are realigned.)

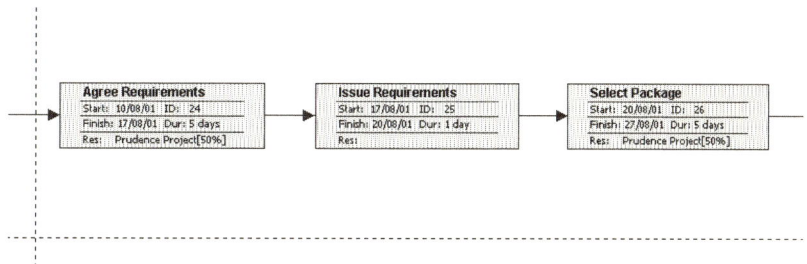

Agree Requirements			Issue Requirements			Select Package		
Start: 10/08/01	ID:	24	Start: 17/08/01	ID:	25	Start: 20/08/01	ID:	26
Finish: 17/08/01	Dur: 5 days		Finish: 20/08/01	Dur: 1 day		Finish: 27/08/01	Dur: 5 days	
Res: Prudence Project[50%]			Res:			Res: Prudence Project[50%]		

Filtering

Project 2000 now lets you apply filters in the Network Diagram view. Filtering works the same in this view as in any other. You can use the Filter by box on the Toolbar to select unstarted tasks, tasks allocated to a resource, etc.

You can also filter the Network Diagram to show all successors to a task.

1   Open your project in Network Diagram view, hold down the shift key and select Task 13 (Produce draft requirements). All the successor tasks (14 to 20) will be selected (shown in black with yellow text).
Zoom out so they are all in view.

2   Drag the split bar (bottom right-hand corner) about half way up the screen. This will create a split-screen view.

3   Click in the lower half of the screen and select View>Gantt Chart from the Menu bar.
The lower half of the screen will now display the Gantt details for the selected tasks in the Network Diagram.
This is a useful compound view which could not be created in earlier versions of Project.

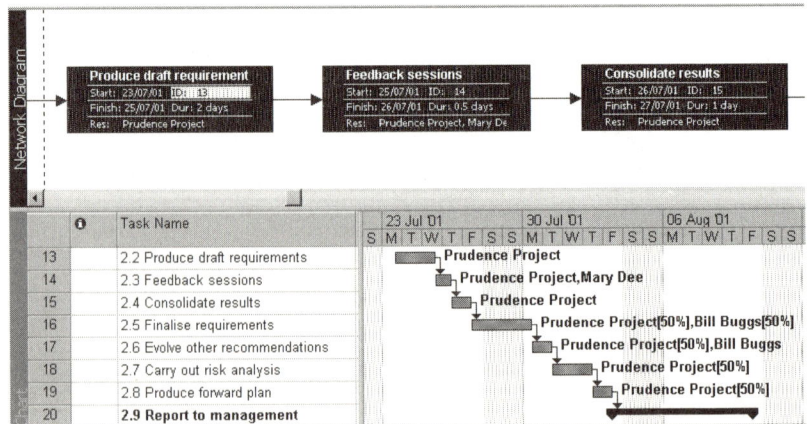

Changing Node Format

Project 2000 gives you control over the number of fields per node, the node shapes and other formatting options. You can specify up to 16 fields per node, change the row heights of cells in the node and change fonts.

In terms of Project 2000, 'white space' means a chart area with no nodes in it.

1 Open your project in Network Diagram view and ensure you have some white space available.

2 Double-click on a blank area of the chart. The Box Styles dialogue box opens:

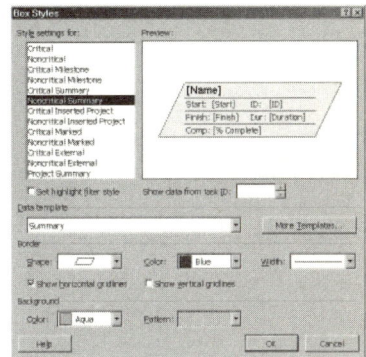

3 Select the different Style Settings to see a preview of the way they are displayed. Click on the Border or Background to make any changes.

4 Click on More Templates and then Edit to open the Data Template definition. Click on the spare cell on the bottom right and select Cost.
Click OK, Close and OK. Summary nodes now include the cost:

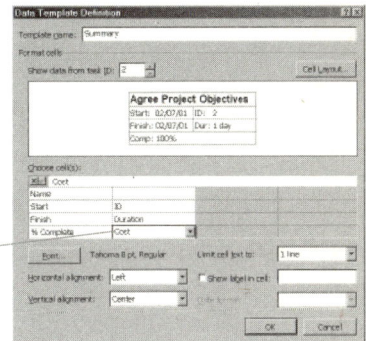

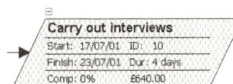

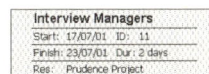

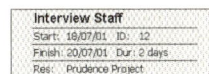

Changing the Layout

Finally you can also change the way that the connecting lines are displayed.

1 Select Format/Layout from the Menu bar. The Layout dialogue box opens:

2 Select Straight. Clear Show page breaks and click OK.

3 Zoom out to view the chart.

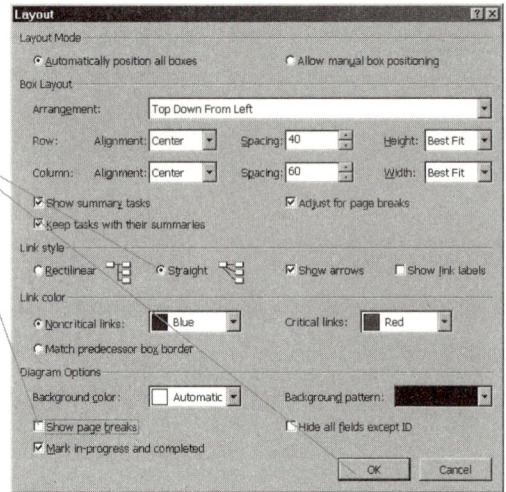

The connectors are now displayed as straight lines and the dotted lines (indicating the page breaks) have been removed.

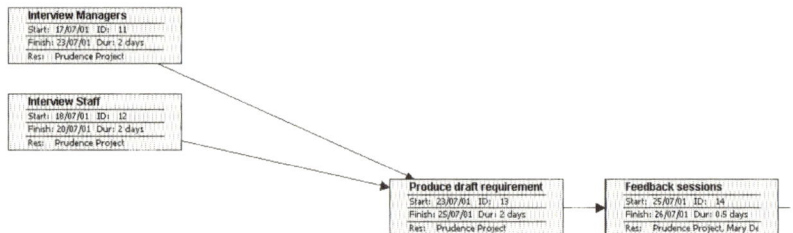

To change the boxes back to show IDs, just double-click on a blank part of the view.

4 Change the layout back so page breaks are displayed and save your project file.

Assigning Resources

You can also deal with assigning resources to a task in Network Diagram view in one of two ways. You can allocate a field in the node box to resource name or resource initials and then type it directly into the field. Alternatively you can use the Task Information dialogue box.

Although we created a new Task 25 (Issue Requirements) in an earlier topic, we have not yet assigned a resource to it.

1 Press F5, type '25' and press Enter to select Task 25 (Issue Requirements) and bring it into view on the chart.

2 Double-click on the task and the Task Information dialogue box opens.
Select the Resources tab and click in the Resource name field.
Click the down arrow, select your project manager and click OK.

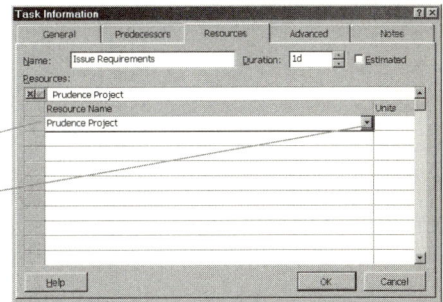

3 Switch back to Gantt Chart view and adjust the timescale to bring the relevant task into view. The task has correctly been assigned to your project manager.

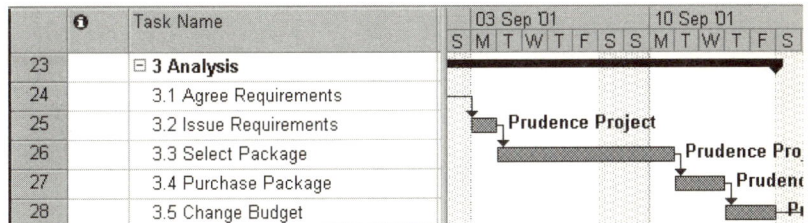

Descriptive Network Diagram

In addition to the basic Network Diagram view there is also a Descriptive Network Diagram. This shows more details of the selected task.

By combining the Network Diagram and Descriptive Network Diagram views you can get more details of the selected nodes.

1 Open your project in Network Diagram view and select Task 13 (Produce Draft Requirements).

2 Move your cursor to the bottom right-hand corner of the screen so that it changes into the split bar symbol:

3 Double-click while the split bar symbol is displayed. The screen splits and the Task Form view is displayed in the lower half of the screen.

4 Click in the lower pane to make it active. Select View/More Views/Descriptive Network Diagram and click Apply.

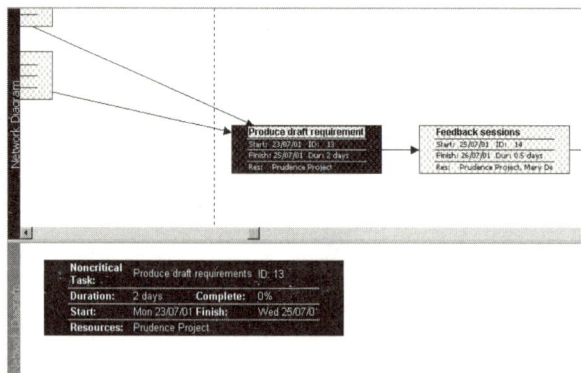

5 Click on different nodes in the top pane and the details are displayed in the lower pane.

Programme Management

This chapter explores the various multiple project environments and shows you how to consolidate projects, share resources and deal with inter-project dependencies.

Covers

Chapter Seventeen

Projects and Programmes

While a project may stand on its own, increasingly, as businesses develop strategic level plans, a project may be a part of a much larger and long term programme consisting of many projects.

In current programme management parlance a 'programme' may consist of a number of 'tranches', which in turn consist of a number of 'projects'. These projects are sometimes grouped together and referred to as a 'project portfolio'.

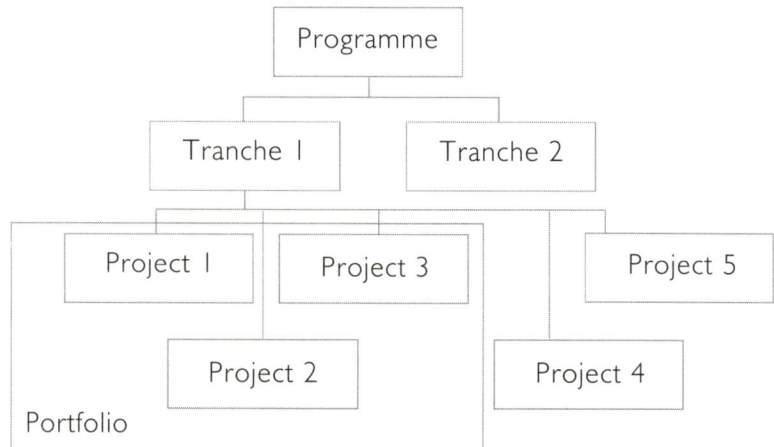

If your project is part of a portfolio, tranche or programme (or you are responsible for managing a portfolio, tranche or programme) your project will not exist in isolation.

Project 2000 provides a way of working with multiple projects that allows you to bring all the projects together to see how they relate. You can work with the individual projects when you need to and then consolidate them together for the big picture.

It also allows you to allocate resources across multiple projects and keep control of them. You can set up one master set of resources and maintain them in one place while still using them on multiple projects. Then if changes occur to the resources, you only have to make them in one place.

Consolidating Projects

If you are responsible for more than one related project, whatever the grouping is called, you can create a consolidated project file to contain them and control them:

You can remove the automatic link if you need to keep the files independent.

1 Open your project file.

2 Now create a new project 'Project 2' and set the start date to 1 September.

3 Create 4 tasks of 20 days' duration (as below), link them and save the project (but don't close it).

	❶	Task Name	Duration	Start	Qtr 3, 2001 Jul Aug Sep	Qtr 4, 2001 Oct Nov Dec
1		Task 1	20 days	Mon 03/09/01		
2		Task 2	20 days	Mon 01/10/01		
3		Task 3	20 days	Mon 29/10/01		
4		Task 4	20 days	Mon 26/11/01		

To select multiple projects hold down Ctrl while you click on each project file.

4 Select Window>New Window from the Menu bar, select both your projects in the dialogue box and click OK.
The consolidated view of the two projects is displayed in a new file.

You can add additional projects using Insert>Project from the Menu bar.

	❶	Task Name	Duration	Start	Qtr 3, 2001	Qtr 4, 2001	Qtr 1, 2002
					Jun Jul Aug Sep	Oct Nov Dec	Jan Feb Mar
1	📋	⊟ **Finance System**	**146 days**	**Mon 02/07/01**			
1		⊞ **Initiation**	**11.88 days**	**Mon 02/07/01**			
9		⊞ **Strategy**	**17.63 days**	**Tue 17/07/01**			
23		⊞ **Analysis**	**25.5 days**	**Fri 10/08/01**			
29		⊞ **Design**	**10 days**	**Mon 17/09/01**			
31		⊞ **Build**	**30 days**	**Mon 01/10/01**			
34		⊞ **Implement**	**51 days**	**Mon 12/11/01**			
2	📋	⊟ **Project2**	**80 days**	**Mon 03/09/01**			
1		Task 1	20 days	Mon 03/09/01			
2		Task 2	20 days	Mon 01/10/01			
3		Task 3	20 days	Mon 29/10/01			
4		Task 4	20 days	Mon 26/11/01			

5 Save the Consolidated project file as 'Consolidate' and answer 'Yes' to save changes to Project 2 and your original project.

Resource Pools

If you are going to have resources working on several projects, you don't want to have to maintain the same resources in more than one place.

Project 2000 allows you to use a resource pool so that you can coordinate the use of the shared resources.

You can either set up a new project file to hold your resource pool or you can designate an existing project as holding the resource pool.

1 Open your original project in Resource Sheet view. The resources are all listed. Don't close the project.

2 Open your new 'Project 2' in Resource Sheet view. There are no resources in the project.

3 Select Tools>Resources>Share Resources from the Menu bar.

4 Select 'Use resources', click the down arrow and select your project from the list. Leave Pool takes precedence selected and click OK.

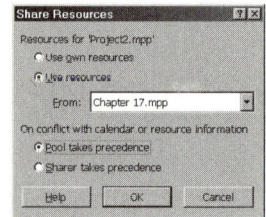

The resource list from the pool (your original project) is now displayed in the Resource Sheet for Project 2.

5 Switch back to your original Project and select Tools>Resources>Share Resources from the Menu bar. The Share Resources dialogue box opens displaying the sharing link to Project 2. Click OK.

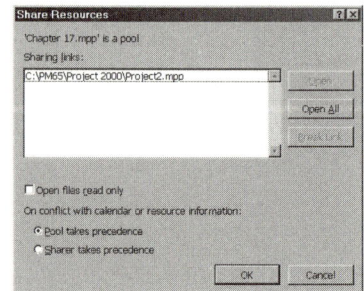

When you open your original project again it will ask you if you want to give write access to other projects, restrict it to the original project or create a separate master resource pool file.

Resolving Over-Allocations

Once you have set up a resource pool and begun sharing resources between several projects you will need to deal with resource over-allocations. Fortunately, it is very similar to dealing with resource over-allocations in a single project.

1   Open your 'Consolidate' project file. The Open Resource Pool dialogue box opens.

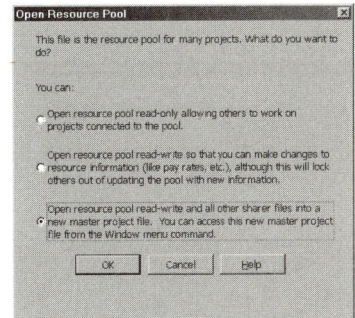

2   Select the third option and click OK. The project file opens together with the linked projects.

3   In Gantt Chart view select Tools>Resource Leveling from the Menu bar, select Manual calculation and click OK.

4   Select Project 2, Task 1 and assign it to your project manager. Switch to Resource Usage view. There is an over-allocation on the project manager.

5   In Gantt Chart view select Tools>Resource Levelling again, select Automatic calculation and click OK. Project 2, Task 1 has been scheduled in and later tasks slipped back on your original project.

When you save the consolidated project file say yes to save the sub-project files as well to keep them in step.

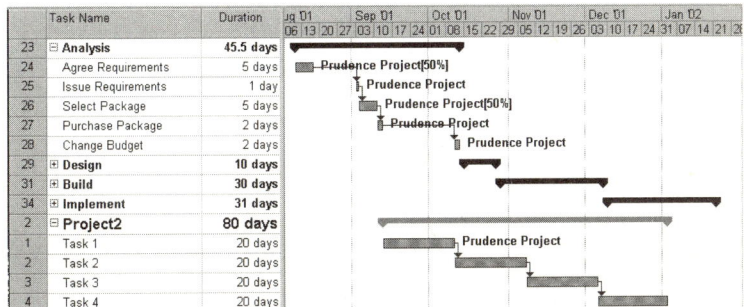

Inter-Project Dependencies

As well as consolidating projects and sharing resources you might have inter-project dependencies. This is where a task in one project is dependent on a task in another project. Dependencies between tasks in different projects can have all the usual dependency types and lag and lead time.

Project 2000 deals with this by creating new pseudo tasks in each of the linked projects that represent the link.

1 Open the consolidated project file and expand the Analysis stage of your original project.

You can also change the start date through the Task Information box.

2 Position your cursor over the Gantt Chart bar for Task 24 (Agree Requirements). The cursor changes to a four-headed arrow symbol.

3 Now drag from Task 24 down to Project 2, Task 1 and release the mouse button. A link is established.

4 Now create a link from Project 2, Task 1 to the task following Task 24 in the original project. Then remove the redundant link between Task 24 and Task 26.

5 Click the Save button and click 'Yes to All' to save the sub-projects.

6 Now switch to (or open) your original project. Notice that Task 1 (from Project 2) has been inserted and is shown in light grey indicating an external task:

If you position your cursor over the external task the details will be displayed. If you double-click it you will switch to the task in Project 2.

	ⓘ	Task Name	Duration	Start	Aug '01 06 13 20 27	Sep '01 03 10 17 24	Oct '01 01 08 15 22	Nov 29 05
23		⊟ **3 Analysis**	**45.5 days**	**Fri 10/08/01**				
24		3.1 Agree Requirements	5 days	Fri 10/08/01	Prudence Project[50%]			
25		3.2 Task 1	20 days	Mon 03/09/01				
26		3.3 Issue Requirements	1 day	Mon 01/10/01			Prudence Project	
27		3.4 Select Package	5 days	Tue 02/10/01			Prudence Pro	
28		3.5 Purchase Package	2 days	Tue 09/10/01			Prudence Pr	
29		3.6 Change Budget	2 days	Thu 11/10/01			Prudence P	
30		⊞ **4 Design**	**10 days**	**Mon 15/10/01**				
32		⊞ **5 Build**	**30 days**	**Mon 29/10/01**				
35		⊞ **6 Implement**	**31 days**	**Mon 10/12/01**				

Project Central

This chapter introduces Project Central, the new companion product to Project 2000. It starts with a brief description of the product, describes how it is accessed, covers some of the main functions and describes the administration module.

Covers

Chapter Eighteen

Project Central

Project Central is a companion product to Project 2000 and consists of two parts, the Server and the Client.

Project Central Server consists of the Internet Information Server (IIS) and the database of project information (which can be held on Oracle, SQL Server or MSDE).

The Client consists of a Web browser (such as Internet Explorer) or the Browser Module for Project Central which is provided with Project Central.

Project Central aims to assist collaborative working between the project manager, project team members and senior management.

Project Manager

Project managers can use Project Central to keep project progress information up to date. They can set up auto-accept features so they can designate what information can be automatically updated and what information they need to review before updating a project. They can request status reports from the other team members, which can be rolled up into one report.

Team Members

Project team members can view a day-by-day work plan and their own task Gantt Chart, enter actual hours worked for project tasks and non-working time and inform their project manager of holidays or other calendar exceptions. With the permission of the project manager, they can also add tasks and delegate tasks to others on the team.

Senior Managers

Project sponsors or senior managers can get a concise view of project information. They can view project summaries and get graphic indicators (traffic lights) to assess the progress of projects. If required they can then drill into the project details as necessary.

Accessing Project Central

Initially project managers need to set up how they want the project team members to access Project Central and if they have the authority to delegate tasks. Once that is done they need to give them the URL of the Server:

1 Start your browser and enter the URL of the Project Central Server. The log-on page is displayed:

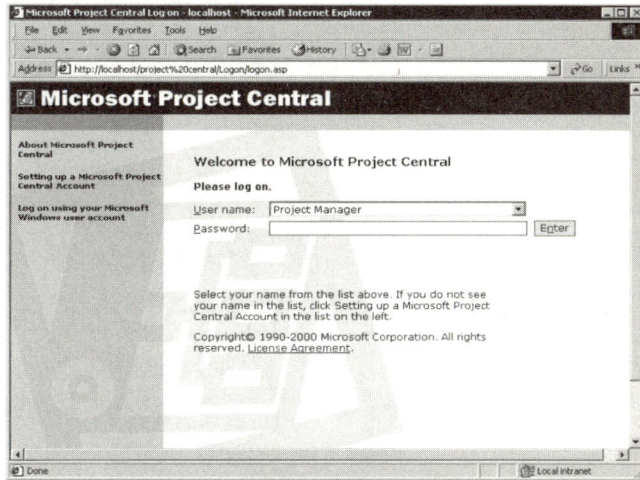

2 Select your user name from the drop down list and enter your password. You will be presented with a home page:

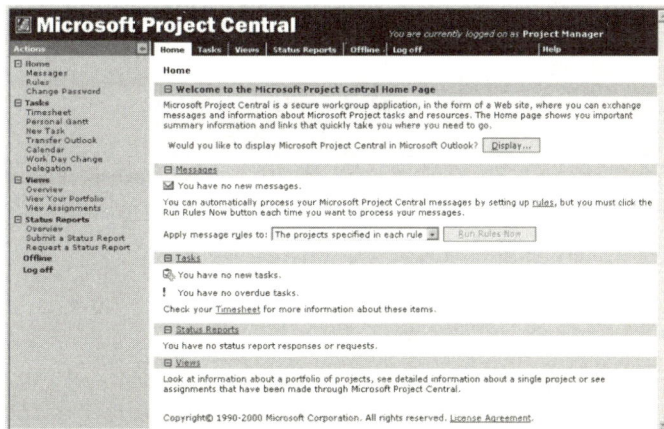

Personal Gantt Charts

Project team members can see their own tasks presented graphically in the Project Central Gantt Chart view. This view can even be customised by reordering the columns, filtering for specific tasks, and grouping by project name, start date, or other task characteristics.

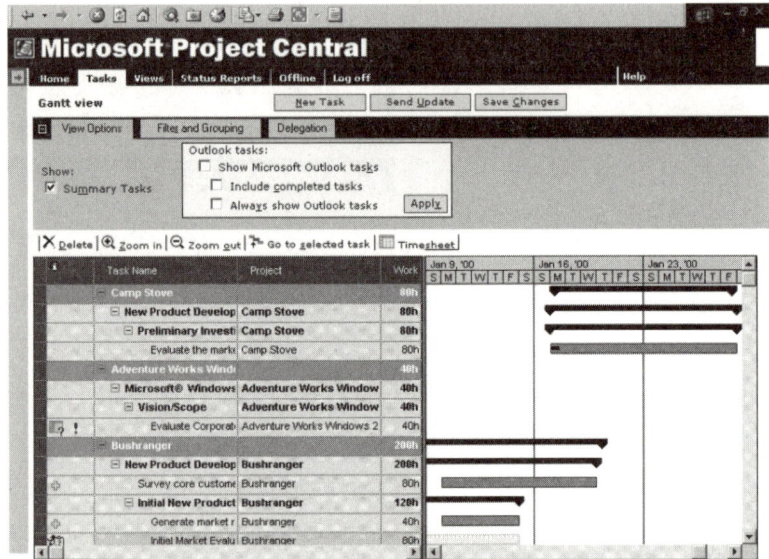

Task Insertion

If a task needs to be inserted into the project, it can be added using the New Task feature, specifying the name of the task, its duration and any comments. New tasks are not updated in the project until the project manager approves them.

Task Delegation

Users can delegate tasks to another team member if they have been authorised to do so. The project manager is automatically notified of all task delegations.

Nonworking Time

Finally users can input non-working time (holidays, training, etc.) which is again reported to the project manager so that it can be added to the master project plan and the relevant tasks rescheduled as required.

Timesheets

From the Project Central Timesheet, users can update actual work, percentage completed or any other field that can be edited (including custom fields) for any task. The information input is sent to the project manager to allow him or her to update the main project with it.

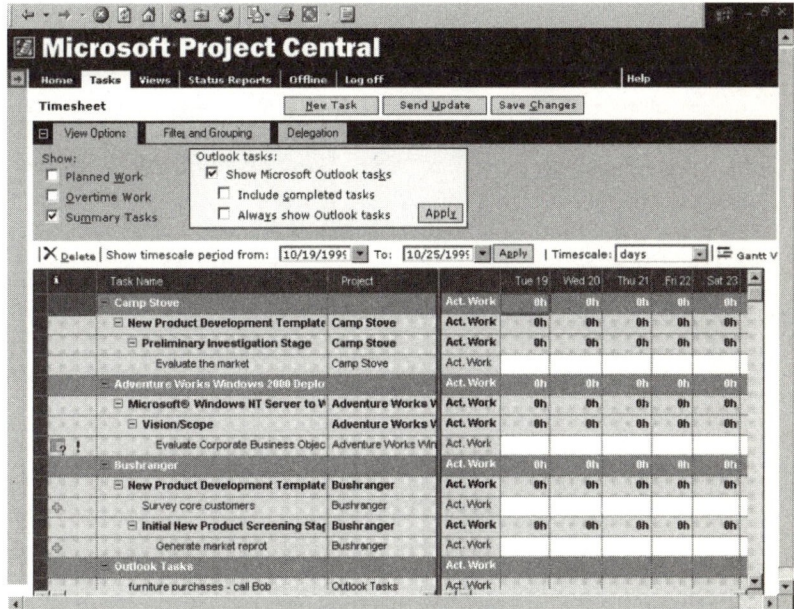

You can filter and group tasks in the timesheet to organise data and see it the way you want. When you enter actual work hours in the grid, the Remaining Work field is automatically reduced. Remaining work can be directly edited from the grid to let the project manager know that the duration of a task has changed.

You can input progress either by actual hours spent on each task or by estimating what percent of the task is complete. This information is then reported to the project manager via Project Central. The project manager can define rules for updating the project plan: with or without review, without review if reported hours are within budgeted hours, etc. These rules can be set based on the contents of any field.

Project Central Views

There are three kinds of views available in Project Central:

View Your Portfolio:

The functions of the various Project Central views are as follows:

- *View Your Portfolio gives a strategic overview of a pre-defined portfolio of projects.*
- *View Your Project shows detailed project information.*
- *View Assignments shows the relationships between resources and tasks.*

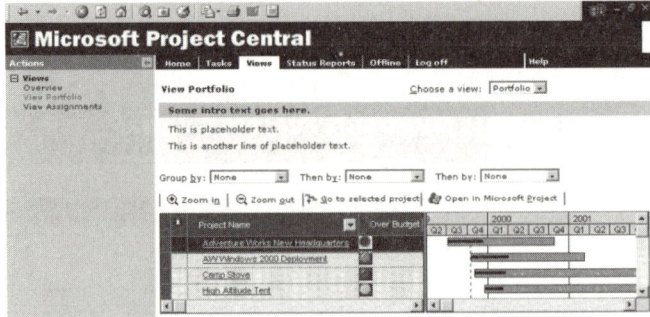

View Your Project:

View Assignments:

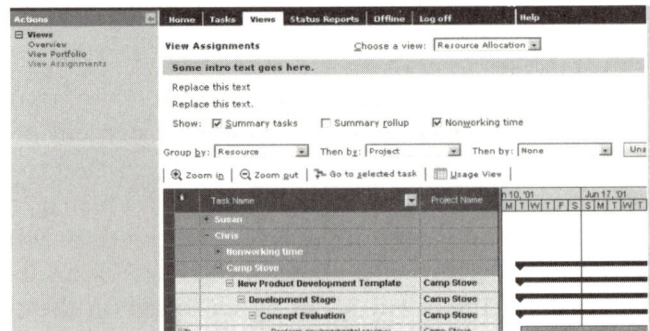

Status Reports

In Project Central you can request custom, text-based status reports and define the format with sections such as Major Achievements or Project Issues. You can insert text prompts to help the project team member fill out the report. You can define regular intervals for the reports to be produced or the requests can be sent out individually. The project team members will have an indicator showing when their status reports are due and a graphical indicator will show if any reports are overdue.

Once the project team members have completed their status reports, Project Central can combine the individual reports into a single group report for the entire team if required. The project manager can decide if the reports are automatically merged or if reports from specific team members need to be reviewed before merging.

This process creates one overall team report showing important information, including who wrote the comments and when, as illustrated in the following example:

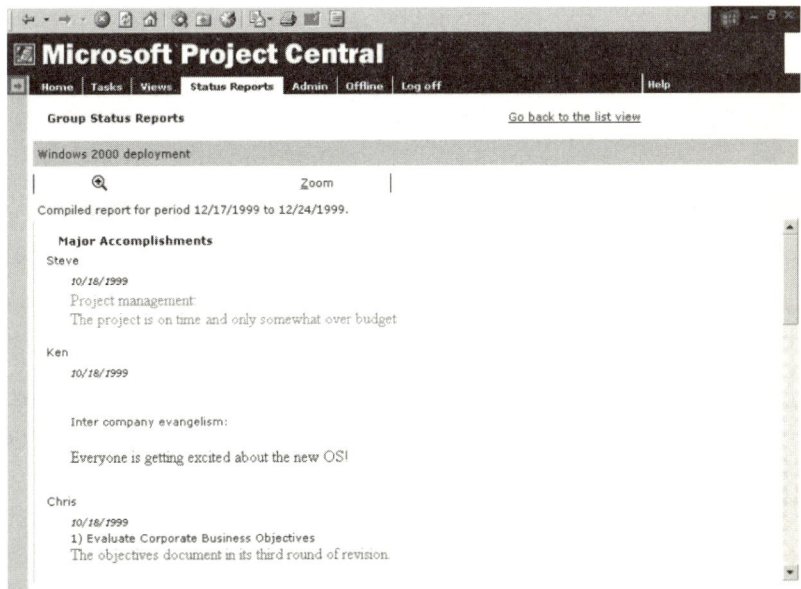

Administration Module

The Administration Module in Project Central allows the project manager or administrator to add and remove user accounts, set database options, clean up the Project Central database and control access to the Project Central site. The administrator can customise the appearance of Project Central pages by adding a company logo or hyperlinks to other Web sites or files.

Non-project time categories such as holidays, illness or work not related to the project are defined here. Once these definitions have been set, this type of time can be tracked along with project time so the project manager has a complete view of each team member's time.

Gantt bar formatting is also done from this module along with security, account creation and definition of categories of people (to enable limited views of project data). A category is a mapping of users to projects and views. For each category, administrators can specify the users that belong to that category, the projects those users can see, and the views with which they can look at the portfolio of projects, individual projects and resource assignment information. Examples of categories include Project Sponsor, Project Manager, Team Manager and Team Member.

Everyone who uses Project Central has a role assigned. By default it is Team Member but the administrator can change the role for any user. Project Central has three key roles:

- *Administrator*: can set up and customise the site, set security, define roles and categories. Has access to all project data.

- *Manager*: can assign tasks, track hours, define status reports. Has access to view projects as set by the administrator.

- *Team Member*: can view tasks, enter work complete, fill out status reports. Has access to view projects set by administrator (by default all projects in which they have assigned tasks).

Advanced Topics

In this chapter we take a look at Earned Value Analysis, customising the Gantt Chart and Toolbars, setting up a workgroup for the project team and using it to allocate work and request status reports.

Covers

Chapter Nineteen

Earned Value Analysis

Earned Value Analysis is a way of measuring project progress in terms of the cost of production.

At the planning stage the total cost of producing each product (deliverable), and therefore the project in total, is produced. This will typically consist of the resource costs plus any other fixed costs (materials, equipment, fees, etc.) which may be incurred. In earned value terms this cost is treated as the value (or worth) of the product.

Earned Value is nothing to do with the benefits of a project, just the costs.

As each product or deliverable is produced (or even part-completed if you wish to measure work in progress), the actual cost of producing it will be known from the time and cost data that you have input for the project.

Using the budget and actual cost, the following three variables are produced:

- *Budgeted Cost of Work Scheduled (BCWS)* – this is the budgeted cost of the work planned to be done in the time being measured. This is the baselined planned expenditure.

- *Budgeted Cost of Work Performed (BCWP)* – this is the budgeted cost of the work that has actually been completed in the time being measured. It is sometimes referred to as the Earned Value as it is what it *should* have cost us to produce the work we have actually completed.

- *Actual Cost of Work Performed (ACWP)* – this is what it has actually cost to perform the work we have actually completed.

Using the above three figures, a number of calculations can be performed to measure progress in cost terms, such as:

In simple terms, any calculation that gives a negative result is not good!

- Schedule Variation = BCWP–BCWS (how much we should have spent to produce what we have, minus planned expenditure).

- Cost Variation = BCWP–ACWP (how much we should have spent, minus what we have actually spent).

Project 2000 has an Earned Value Report and an Earned Value Resource Table. You can also export earned value data to a spreadsheet such as Excel to produce more sophisticated charts and graphs.

1   Open your project in Gantt Chart view, display all tasks for the first two phases then select Project>Project Information from the Menu bar. In the Project Information dialogue box set the Status date to the date you have input actual data to (09/07/01).

2   Select View>Reports>Costs>Earned Value Report. The Earned Value report is produced:

Earned Value as of Wed 09.07.01
Finance System

ID	Task Name	BCWS	BCWP	ACWP	SV	CV
2	Agree Project Objectives	£160.00	£160.00	£160.00	£0.00	£0.00
3	Identify Stakeholders	£160.00	£160.00	£160.00	£0.00	£0.00
4	Identify Project Team	£480.00	£480.00	£480.00	£0.00	£0.00
5	Identify Business Case	£400.00	£400.00	£400.00	£0.00	£0.00
6	Analyse the Risks	£165.00	£140.25	£202.50	-£24.75	-£62.25
7	Produce Outline Project Plan	£160.00	£0.00	£0.00	-£160.00	£0.00
8	Project Approval	£0.00	£0.00	£0.00	£0.00	£0.00
11	Interview Managers	£0.00	£0.00	£0.00	£0.00	£0.00
12	Interview Staff	£0.00	£0.00	£0.00	£0.00	£0.00
13	Produce draft requirements	£0.00	£0.00	£0.00	£0.00	£0.00
14	Feedback sessions	£0.00	£0.00	£0.00	£0.00	£0.00
15	Consolidate results	£0.00	£0.00	£0.00	£0.00	£0.00
16	Finalise requirements	£0.00	£0.00	£0.00	£0.00	£0.00
17	Evolve other recommendations	£0.00	£0.00	£0.00	£0.00	£0.00
18	Carry out risk analysis	£0.00	£0.00	£0.00	£0.00	£0.00
19	Produce forward plan	£0.00	£0.00	£0.00	£0.00	£0.00
21	Prepare Report	£0.00	£0.00	£0.00	£0.00	£0.00
22	Present to Management	£0.00	£0.00	£0.00	£0.00	£0.00
		£1,525.00	£1,340.25	£1,402.50	-£184.75	-£62.25

3   To use the Earned Value Table switch to Resource Usage view, select View>Table>More Tables>Earned Value from the Menu bar and click Apply.

4   To export Earned Value date for use in a spreadsheet select File>Save As from the Menu bar. Click the Save as type down arrow and select Microsoft Excel Workbook (or CSV for other spreadsheets). Click Save and the Export Mapping dialogue box opens. Select Earned Value Information and click Save. Your earned value data is saved in the required format for you to open in your spreadsheet.

Customising the Gantt Chart

There are a number of things that you can customise on the Gantt Chart (and indeed on other views as well) to make it look the way that you want. The colour and style of the various elements that appear on the schedule can be changed along with the font of any text.

I   Open your project in Gantt Chart view and Show All Sub-Tasks. Note the summary tasks are all displayed in bold.

2   Select the task ID field of Task 1 (Initiation) and click the Bold button on the Toolbar to turn it off. The text is now displayed as normal text. Select the other summary tasks and turn bold off.

B

You can select multiple items by holding down Ctrl.

3   Select Format>Bar Styles from the Menu bar. The Bar Styles dialogue box opens.

Scroll down to External Tasks (currently a grey solid bar), select it and change the pattern and colour of the middle bar to lines and olive. Click OK and external Task 25 (Task 1 from Project 2) is now displayed in the new style.

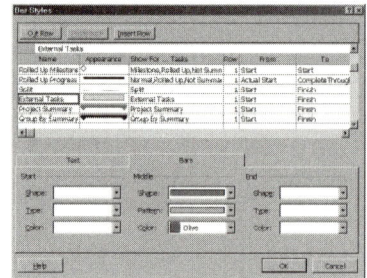

4   Select View>Toolbars>Drawing to open the Drawing Toolbar and click the Text Box button.

5   Drag to create a box to the left of Task 21, type 'Project 2 involvement for Project Manager' and click outside the box.

	O	Task Name	Duration	Start	Jul 01	Aug 01	Sep 01	O
23		⊟ 3 Analysis	45.5 days	Fri 10/08/01				
24		3.1 Agree Requirements	5 days	Fri 10/08/01			Prudence Project 50%	
25		3.2 Task 1	20 days	Mon 03/09/01	Project 2			
26		3.3 Issue Requirements	1 day	Mon 01/10/01	involvement for			
27		3.4 Select Package	5 days	Tue 02/10/01	Project Manager			

Custom Toolbars

Toolbar buttons provide quick access to frequently used menu items. In Project 2000 you can create your own custom toolbars, to put all the buttons you often use in one place. You can also create your own buttons for new items. Toolbars are saved in the global template: once you've created a new toolbar you can use it in any new projects.

1 Select View>Toolbars>Customise from the Menu bar. The Customize dialogue box opens and lists all toolbars. It also has tabs for the commands and display options.

After step 2, the new toolbar isn't much to look at yet but we will add buttons to it in later steps!

2 Click New, type 'Custom Toolbar' in the name and click OK. The new toolbar is added to the list and a blank toolbar appears that looks like this:

3 Drag the new toolbar away from the Customize dialogue box, click the Commands tab and select the View category. The View buttons and commands are displayed. Drag Toolbars from Commands and drop it on your custom toolbar.

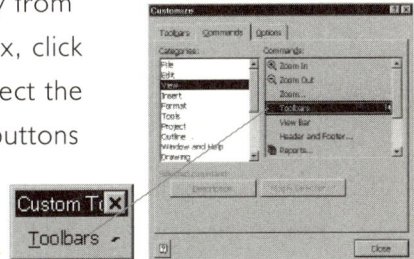

4 Now drag 'Reports' to the custom toolbar, then click Project category and add 'Project Information'. Click Close on the Customize dialogue box. Your new Toolbar buttons are all active – try them!

You can add any buttons or commands to your toolbar and organise it exactly how you want it using customisation.

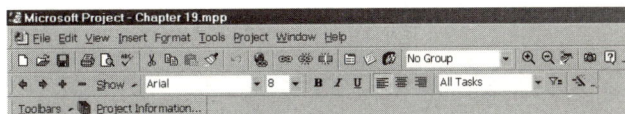

5 Drag your new toolbar and drop it below the existing Toolbars. It should look like this.

Workgroups

If you have an e-mail system you can set up a workgroup in Project 2000 which will allow you to keep in touch with your team by e-mail.

For an e-mail workgroup to be set up the project manager and the rest of the project team (workgroup) must meet three requirements:

1.   Connection to a network or the Internet

2.   Use of a MAPI-compliant, 32-bit e-mail system

3.   Installation of WGsetup.exe on their computers

The project manager must have Project 2000 installed on his/her computer but it is not necessary for the other members of the workgroup.

Configure a Workgroup for E-Mail

1   Select Tools > Options from the Menu bar, select the Workgroup tab, select E-mail in the Default workgroup messaging. (If you want this to apply to all new projects click Set as Default.)

2   Select the General tab, type your name in the User name box and click OK.

3   To add e-mail addresses for team members select View > Resource Sheet then View > Table > Entry.

4   Select a resource name and click the Resource Information button on the toolbar. Select the General tab, type in their e-mail address and click OK. Repeat step 4 for each member of the workgroup.

You can also get the Resource Information dialogue box by double-clicking on the resource name.

Allocating Assignments

Once the workgroup is set up the project manager can assign tasks and request status updates from the workgroup team members. The team members can respond and send notes.

1   Open your project and select View>Toolbars>Workgroup from the Menu bar to open the Workgroup Toolbar:

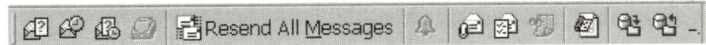

2   Select Task 21 (Prepare Report), click the Team Assign (left-hand) button, select Send message for selected task and click OK. The Team Assign dialogue box opens. Change the subject to 'Confirm Assignment' and click Send. The message is sent and an e-mail symbol is added to the Information field.

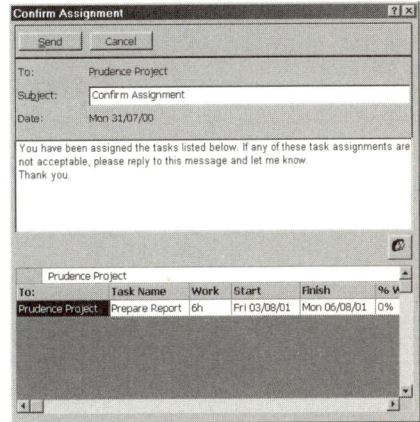

3   Pause your cursor over the Information field to display the status message:

	🛈	Task Name	Duration	Start
20		⊟ 2.9 Report to management	5.13 days	Fri 03/08/01
21		2.9.1 Prepare Report	1.5 days	Fri 03/08/01
22		There has not yet been a response to all the TeamAssign messages for this task.	0.5 days	Fri 10/08/01
23			45.5 days	Fri 10/08/01
24		3.1 Agree Requirements	5 days	Fri 10/08/01

Keeping In Touch

As the project progresses and things change you will need to keep the team in touch with things. Workgroup Messaging contains a number of functions to help with this such as Team Update, Team Status, Resend All Messages and Send As Attachment.

Team Update

1   Select Tools>Workgroup>Team Update from the Menu bar (or click the Team Update button on the Workgroup Toolbar). The message dialogue box opens.

2   Type the subject, message and any comments and click Send.

Resend All Messages

From time to time you may need to resend some or all of the tasks assigned to a particular resource or to the whole team:

1   In Gantt Chart view select the tasks that you want to resend (if not all tasks).

2   Select Tools>Workgroup>Resend All Messages. Select All tasks or Selected tasks as appropriate. The message dialogue box opens.

3   Type the subject, the text of your message, any comments and click Send.

Send As Attachment

To send the project file as an e-mail attachment:

1   Click the 'Send to Mail Recipient (as Attachment)' button on the Workgroup Toolbar.

2   Type the recipient, any message and click Send.

Status Reporting

As well as being able to allocate assignments to the workgroup, you can also request and submit status reports by e-mail or over the Web.

Requesting a Status Report

1 Open your project and in Project Information change the status date to 20/07/01.

2 Select Task 6 (Analyse the Risks) and Task 7 (Produce Outline Project Plan).

3 Click the Team Status button on the Workgroup Toolbar.
The Team Status dialogue box appears with the selected tasks and assigned resources:

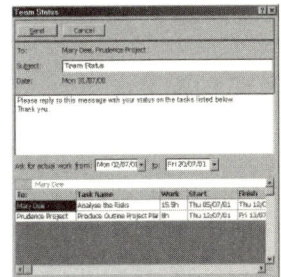

4 Make any changes required to the subject, message, etc. and click Send. The message is sent and the Information field on both tasks is updated with a symbol.

Submitting a Status Report

1 On receipt of the Team Status Request message, enter the actual work performed for the period, the estimated work remaining for the task and any comments.

Remaining Work	2/7	3/7	4/7	5/7	6/7	7/7	8/7	9/7	10/7
8h								6h	2h
8h	0h	0h	0h	0h	0h	0h	0h	6h	2h

2 Type any required message in the Message box and click Send. Your status report is submitted.

Templates

Project 2000 now allows you to base a project on a template and provides a number of standard templates for you to use. You can also create custom templates.

1. Close any open project files and select File>New from the Menu bar.
   The New dialogue box opens. Select the Project Templates tab.

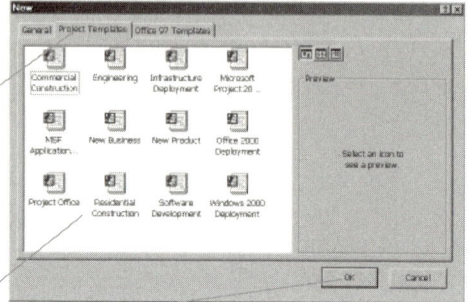

2. Select the project template you wish to use and click OK. The Project Information dialogue box opens for the start date etc. and the file is created based on the template.

Creating Custom Templates

It is equally straightforward to create your own custom templates from an existing project file:

1. Open your project in Gantt Chart view and select File>Save As from the Menu bar. The Save As dialogue box opens.

2. Select Save as type: Template and select the directory where your Project 2000 templates are stored (typically C:\Program Files\Microsoft Office\Templates\1033) and click Save. The Save As template dialogue box opens.

3. Select any of the data you want to be cleared from the template (baseline values, actual values, etc.) and click Save. You can now create a new project based on this template.

HOT TIP

You can find where your template files are by selecting Tools>Options>Save from the Menu bar.

HOT TIP

Also you will probably need to clear any constraints.

Myth and Methodology

In this chapter we take a final look at some project management methodologies and how they might help (or possibly hinder) you in the effective management of your project.

Covers

Chapter Twenty

Project Methodologies

While Project 2000 provides an excellent project planning and scheduling tool, it will only be effective if it is used within the context of a properly managed project.

Project Management is a large subject and this book does not claim to be the last word on it! However, we have attempted to include some hints and tips on good project management practice where applicable.

This chapter is intended to give an overview of some of the methodologies that are available to assist in your project management. The methodologies included have all proven to work well with Project 2000.

If you work for a larger organisation (or even a smaller one that is focused on strategy) you are quite likely to have some project management standards and methodologies in place. If so, you should use them together with Project 2000 to manage your project. If not then this chapter may help.

What Are Project Methodologies?

Project methodologies tend to fall into two main groups: Project Management methodologies and Systems Development methodologies. The former are applicable to all projects, whatever their objectives. The latter are only applicable to computer systems development projects. It is not possible to cover all the methodologies currently available, but this chapter covers four of the major ones in current use. What the methodologies set out to do is help you manage the function, time and cost forces acting on your project.

The forces are also stated as Quality, Time and Cost. In this context Quality and Functionality are interchangeable.

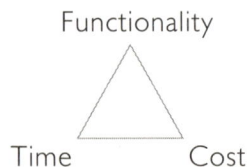

Functionality

Time   Cost

Changing any one will impact either or both of the others. For instance, if you increase the functionality of the project it will either take longer or cost more (or both).

The four methodologies and their background and use are as follows:

PRINCE 2

PRINCE has proved to be one of the most successful and popular project management methodologies. With the introduction of version 2, all reference to computer development was removed and the methodology became truly generic. It is suitable for any type of project and has been well proven in practice.

Oracle CASE*Method

The Oracle CASE*Method is again a project management methodology, but in contrast to PRINCE, Oracle's methodology assumes that the project is to develop or purchase computer software. However, despite this assumption, it can still be used with equal success on non-computer projects.

SSADM

Structured System Analysis and Design Method (SSADM) is exactly what it says. It is highly structured and focuses on the Analysis and Design stages of computer systems development projects. In fact it covers these stages in great detail. It also uses the traditional waterfall approach (sometimes referred to as the cascade method) to systems development. In this approach the requirements (functionality) are frozen early in the project and the approach is rigid. One stage cannot begin until the previous stage has been completed and signed off.

DSDM

Dynamic Systems Development Method (DSDM) represents current thinking about the most effective way to develop a business system. In this approach the requirements (functionality) are only agreed at a very strategic business level and are allowed to develop dynamically through the analysis, design and build stages of the project. It achieves this through the use of prototypes and business models.

SSADM

The Structured Systems Analysis and Design Method (SSADM) is the UK government's standard method for carrying out the systems analysis and design stages of an information technology (IT) project. It breaks them into five modules and seven discrete stages:

Feasibility Study (FS)
Stage 0 – Feasibility (not really part of the project)

Requirements Analysis (RA)
Stage 1 – Investigation of Current Environment
Stage 2 – Business Systems Options

Requirements Specification (RS)
Stage 3 – Specification of Definition of Requirements

Logical Systems Specification (LS)
Stage 4 – Technical System Options
Stage 5 – Logical Design

Physical Design (PD)
Stage 6 – Physical Design

By taking this approach the requirements are gradually evolved and agreed and frozen by stage 3. The system is then designed in detail through the next 3 stages.

The advantages of this approach are: a) there will be fewer unknown factors so estimates of time and cost are likely to be more accurate; b) it is possible to contract out discrete work packages as there will be well documented requirements; and c) it is well suited to fixed, well-known requirements.

The disadvantages are: a) it is rigid and does not allow for requirements to develop through the project; and b) it tends to be long-winded and can extend the duration of a project compared to other methodologies.

It represents the fixed functionality approach, so cost and time are the variables that can be changed.

DSDM

The Dynamic Systems Development method (DSDM) is a Rapid Application Development (RAD) methodology. It is more or less the exact opposite of the SSADM approach. In DSDM the Time is fixed, the Cost (of resources) is fixed as much as possible and the Functionality (requirements) that will be met is allowed to change.

It uses five stages which map onto the traditional project stages as follows:

Feasibility Study
Not really part of the project but this is where the decision to adopt a RAD approach has to be taken. It is a pre-project activity.

Business Study
This is traditionally the Strategy Stage which identifies and baselines the high-level (strategic) business requirements.

Functional Model Iteration
This is traditionally the Analysis Stage which fleshes out the requirements by producing iterative prototypes.

Design and Build Iteration
This is traditionally two stages: the Design Stage (which determines how the requirements will be met) and the Build Stage (which carries it out). This stage develops the prototypes into final products and produces their documentation.

Implementation
This is the same as the traditional Implementation Stage.

The advantages are: a) real business requirements are delivered in the shortest time; and b) costs are usually controlled because of the fixed timescale.

The disadvantages are: a) it will not work well in rigid organisations; and b) it needs fully committed users with the ability to make business decisions (but perhaps this is an advantage!).

PRINCE 2

PRINCE stands for PRojects IN Controlled Environments. It does not concern itself with what the project is about, just how it is managed. It defines a project management structure and project management processes (tasks and activities) and products (deliverables) that will work with any project.

The main processes are:

Start Up the Project (SU)
This is actually just a short pre-project activity.

Initiate the Project (IP)
The first stage of the project which formally gets it under way and plans it (Initiation Stage).

Control the Stage (CS)
This process together with the next one is carried out for each of the other stages of the project. Whether it is just one stage (Do It); the traditional Analysis, Design, Build and Implement Stages; the DSDM Stages or just periods of time.

Manage Stage Boundaries (SB)
Deals with the stage approval and start activities.

Close the Project (CP)
These are supplemented by three other processes:

- *Direct the Project (DP)* – this defines the project board or sponsor's role.

- *Planning (PL)* –takes place during SU, IP and MP.

- *Manage Product Delivery (MP)* – defines how the actual work production is controlled.

The PRINCE 2 methodology is flexible enough to work with any of the other three methodologies covered in the chapter or indeed any other development, study or construction methodology.

Oracle CASE*Method

Computer Aided System Engineering (CASE) was a term coined to cover the automation of systems design and development. It includes both the tools (design, modelling and prototyping) and the approach (methodology). Oracle developed their CASE*Method to complement their CASE tool products but it is completely independent of them and is a methodology in its own right.

There are two reasons for including it in this chapter. Firstly, it represents an excellent example of the traditional approach to project management. Secondly, it is widely used.

It defines the following project stages:

Strategy
The objective of the Strategy Stage is to produce a set of business models (requirements) with a plan of how they will be developed.

Analysis
The Analysis Stage determines what has to be done in order to meet the business requirements (but not yet how).

Design
The Design Stage works out how it is to be done and how the business requirements will be met.

Build
This is the traditional 'Do It' stage. The new system, whatever it is, will be constructed or built.

User Documentation
Traditionally this is part of the Build Stage but this methodology treats it as a separate but parallel stage.

Transition
This is the traditional Implementation Stage.

The method also specifies in detail the tasks, activities and deliverables. It is technical rather than project management.

The Final Word

Putting it all together, Project 2000 is an excellent project planning, scheduling and monitoring tool. By adding the appropriate project management processes or methodologies you really can stay in control of your project.

PRINCE 2 gives an excellent framework for management and a quality focus for a project. It (or sometimes a subset of it) is becoming mandatory in an increasing number of organisations. It defines a project start up and initiation stage better than any of the other methodologies.

SSADM is a mandatory requirement in some government (and quasi-government) organisations. If so, you will need to use it. If not, it is probably best avoided.

Oracle CASE*Method may well be in use in organisations that use the Oracle DBMS (DataBase Management System) although the two are completely freestanding. It contains a useful list of tasks, activities and deliverables for all the major project stages (except Initiation).

DSDM is now well established and based on proven principles. It is an excellent approach to the rapid development of computer systems that really will meet business needs.

So there you go. If you have a free choice or are involved in a non-IT project, have a look at PRINCE. If you are running a systems development project PRINCE + DSDM provide an excellent blend of formal management and a flexible approach. For package selection PRINCE + CASE*Method should cover everything you need. Finally if you have to use SSADM it does at least work with PRINCE!

Murphy's 4th Law

The light at the end of the tunnel will probably turn out to be the headlamp of an oncoming train!

Index